Pu 24-25

DEEP CONVERSION/DEEP PRAYER

THOMAS DUBAY, S.M.

Deep Conversion/ Deep Prayer

IGNATIUS PRESS   SAN FRANCISCO

Cover art: © John and Lisa Merrill / Corbis

Cover design by Riz Boncan Marsella

© 2006 Ignatius Press, San Francisco
All rights reserved
ISBN 978-1-58617-117-9 (PB)
ISBN 978-1-68149-131-8 (eBook)
Library of Congress Control Number 2005933370
Printed in the United States of America ∞

*"Your first duty as pastors
is not projects and organizations,
but to lead your people to a deep intimacy
with the Trinity."*

—John Paul II
to the Austrian bishops

CONTENTS

Abbreviations 9

1. Getting a Feel 11
2. The Radical Conversion 21
3. Degrees of Depth 29
4. Call to the Heights 41
5. A Remarkable Resistance 47
6. Relevance and Motivation 55
7. Conversion and Genuine Love 67
8. Conflicts and Conversion 77
9. A Surefire Program 91
10. The Sacramental Dimension 109

Postscript 121
Bibliography 123

ABBREVIATIONS

AMC   *Ascent of Mt. Carmel*

EPB   *Evidential Power of Beauty*

FW   *Fire Within*

JB   *The Jerusalem Bible*

LG   *Lumen gentium*, Constitution on the Church (Vatican Council II)

NCE   *The New Catholic Encyclopedia*

SC   *Sacrosanctum concilium*, Constitution on the Liturgy (Vatican Council II)

TLG   *Treatise on the Love of God*

I

GETTING A FEEL

If someone interested in trivia was to ask me to name the ten historical persons who have had the greatest impact on my life (aside, of course, from the Lord and his Mother), my list would include Saints Augustine, Thomas Aquinas, Teresa of Avila, John of the Cross, together with John Henry Newman and Hans Urs von Balthasar. To determine the other four might take a bit more pondering, but among them would surely be the man with whom we shall begin our reflections: Saint Bernard of Clairvaux.

This doctor of the Church, a man of towering talent, brilliant mind and golden eloquence, traveled about Europe at the behest of the pope as a highly gifted troubleshooter. But more important than his natural gifts was his sanctity. At about the age of twenty he entered the Cistercian order, bringing thirty other men along with him. Most of us entering a religious community bring no one but ourselves. The monks recognized the youngster early on as a highly unusual newcomer and before long elected him as abbot. Bernard united among his many talents fearlessness and tenderness, a rare combination. The most touching funeral homily I have ever read or heard was the one he delivered at the death of his blood brother. The saint was a man of profoundly deep prayer and love for God—which, of course, translated, as it always does, into a genuine love for the people in his life.

A fine biographer of Bernard details for about six hundred pages the drift of this paragraph, but we will get to our immediate point without further ado.

The young abbot was speaking to his community one day, and he made a remark that shocked me on my first reading of it. "There are more people converted from mortal sin to grace, than there are religious converted from good to better." Over the years the more I have experienced of life and thought about this statement the more I have been convinced of its truth. Yet one may ask, what is so shocking about it?

Before responding to this question, it may be helpful to unpack the implications of this plain fact. What Bernard said of religious unfortunately is true in all states of life: bishops, priests, married men and women. Routine daily experience bears it out. Like any competent speaker, the saint wanted to be clear and direct, and so he spoke of the men in front of him. Yet we may wonder: what is shocking about this prosaic but seldom discussed truth?

Putting the saint's observation in simple contemporary terms may help. Bernard was saying that there are more men who give up serious alienation from God, mortal sin, than there are people who give up small wrongs, willed venial sins. And there are even fewer who grow into heroic virtue and live as saints live. If we are not saddened by this realization, we ought to be. We need to notice the title of this book: Deep Conversion/Deep Prayer. The twice repeated adjective is important. Seldom explained, it is what we are about here.

Yet a bit more unpacking is needed. A large part of the sadness is the expectation that anyone who basically loves another (real sacrificing love, not mere attraction) in important matters (for example, a husband loving his wife), would naturally go on to love her in smaller ones. I would assume that he would stop being grouchy and abrupt and harsh, that he would be at pains to be kind and gentle, patient and forgiving. I would assume the same in her behavior toward him.

A step further: We would suppose that a person who realistically and fundamentally loves God would be at pains to avoid all smaller offenses against him: gossiping, laziness, overeating, as well as the venial sins mentioned in our previous paragraph—and myriads of other minor wrongs. A third step of unpacking: Most of us would like to think that this person would go on to prove his love further even to the point of total self-giving, even under the duress, hardships and sacrifices entailed in persevering in heroic holiness. But everyone knows that such is unhappily a rare occurrence in the human family. Something is amiss—and on a large scale. Yes, if everything were normal in society, deep conversion would be common, and life would be incomparably happier for everyone. Much more about that as we proceed in our task.

What Is Moral Conversion?

To a goodly number of people the idea of moral conversion is heavily negative, even threatening. It suggests giving up fun things, making sacrifices, cutting down and cutting out, getting rid of numerous selfishnesses. This reaction is understandable, but it is only the smaller aspect of a larger and liberating truth.

An accurate synonym for conversion, as we are using the word here, would be transformation. Put simply, conversion is a basic and marked improvement on the willing level of the human person. Even more pointedly, it is a fundamental change in our willed activities from bad to good, from good to better, and from better to best. Anyone who is fully alive will find this a stimulating set of ideas. We can put the matter in still another way. Conversion is a change from vice to virtue: from deceit and lying to honesty and truth . . . gluttony to temperance . . . vanity to humility . . . lust to love . . . avarice to generosity . . . rage to patience . . . laziness to zeal . . . ugliness to beauty.

From the point of view of attention to and intimacy with God, supreme Beauty, supreme Delight, conversion includes a change from little or no prayer to a determined practice of christic meditation leading eventually to contemplative intimacy, "pondering the word day and night", leading to a sublime "gazing on the beauty of the Lord" with all its varying depths and intensities (Ps 1:1-2; 27:4).

In all of secular literature there is nothing that approaches the literary excellence and the touching tenderness of the parable of the prodigal son, a matchless portrayal of conversion and forgiveness. If the reader notices and ponders the small details of this masterpiece, he finds the divine handwriting throughout the narrative. One verse may exemplify what we mean by this high praise. The egocentric son, having wasted half of his father's fortune with prostitutes, finally comes to his senses, renounces his sins and decides to return to his father. We are then struck with the extraordinary welcome he receives: "While he was still a long way off, his father saw him and was moved with pity. He ran to the boy, clasped him in his arms and kissed him tenderly" (Lk 15:20 JB). Not a single word of reproach—the sinner had already repented. Music, dancing and feasting follow. This scene with its touching tenderness and complete forgiveness is nothing short of divine. The son has been restored to life. He has been transformed, converted and healed. This passage from ugly egocentrism to divinized altruism is a literary and theological gem profoundly instructive for each of us.

Our task in these pages is to reflect upon and absorb what divine revelation has to say about this fundamental conversion and its more profound depths: how can our lives be completely transformed from ugliness to beauty and personal fulfillment?

Human Excellences

Normal people instinctively seek to excel at least in small ways. Little boys skipping stones at a lake shore will spontaneously shout, if anyone is noticing, "Look, I can make a stone skip more times than he can." We all enjoy winning at a game of cards or sports—or even finishing a crossword puzzle completely.

There are two kinds of human excellence, the first of which is on the level of natural talents, gifts, accomplishments. These occur in many areas and to differing degrees: intelligence, scholarship, literature, music, art, sports. The second and higher type lies on the level of personal goodness, integrity, virtue, sanctity. Here we find the beauties of selfless love, humility, honesty, patience, chastity, fidelity, generosity.

It is immediately obvious that someone can be eminent in the first area of talents and accomplishments and yet a moral wretch in the second. There are the few who excel on both levels: Augustine, Thomas Aquinas, Catherine of Siena, Teresa of Avila. It should be obvious to a consistent theist that to be a saint is immeasurably more important than to be a world class scholar, violinist or an olympic gold medalist. In these pages we are concerned with conversion through all the degrees of growth in the virtues and prayer depth that lead up to the transformation of the human person as a person, from one beauty to another still more lofty (2 Cor 3:18).

Kinds of Conversion

Hence we are not here concerned chiefly with changing from atheism to theism or from one religion to another —absolutely basic as these are. What we directly envision are moral and spiritual developments for the better: giving up mortal and venial sins, loving and serving God and our neighbors more and more perfectly, growing in a deepening prayer intimacy with the indwelling Trinity.

There are several ways in which moral conversions can occur. We find in the history of the Church sudden and profoundly powerful experiences of God that instantaneously change a person for the better. Unexpectedly, rapidly, these experiences can convince an individual of the truth of divine revelation together with a powerful desire to live it out. There was Saint Paul on the road to Damascus and Saint Augustine in the garden. Closer to our own day André Frossard, an atheist, while in a church, received in an instant a powerful light convincing him of the truth of Catholicism. He later wrote that what he learned in that one moment about the Church and her teaching would fill ten volumes.

Then there are conversions that happen rapidly, even if not in an instant. I think of the teenage girl in the atheistic Soviet Union who somehow came into the possession of the Gospel of Luke, read it, and then said, "I fell in love with Him" (Jesus). Many of us know of the philosopher Edith Stein who read the autobiography of Saint Teresa of Jesus (Teresa of Avila) in the course of one evening, put the book down and declared: "This is the truth." A keen minded intellectual was immediately convinced that only God through his Church could produce so magnificent a woman. I myself knew firsthand of a young man who, while a university student on a secular campus, after listening to one homily, then and there decided to become a Catholic. Now in this last case it is possible that considerable thought had preceded this decision. But it seemed from the firsthand account that his decision was triggered by evidence he found absolutely convincing on the spot.

More commonly the path to truth and moral goodness is gradual. Deepening insight, earnest study, continuing moral growth combine with divine grace to open new vistas to the sincere inquirer. Thousands each year attend parish instruction classes especially suited to their needs and desires. But especially fascinating are the accounts of searching and finding that intellectual giants have left us. John Henry Newman and G. K. Chesterton, each in his own unique way, have favored posterity with eloquent and penetrating descriptions of their long and arduous searching through studies of Scripture, history, philosophy and theology—as well as enemies of the Church. One might think that the latter, the foes of Catholicism, would have dissuaded these brilliant minds from further investigations. On the contrary, the typical shallowness of their attacks and often mutually contradictory objections all the more convinced these two Englishmen that indeed they were on the right track. And neither man later regretted for a moment the decision he finally made.

Joseph Pearce, in his book *Literary Converts*, narrates captivating accounts of how keen and honest minds find ultimate truth. In addition to Newman and Chesterton, we may suggest a few of the many prominent intellectuals who in our modern period have entered the Church from Britain alone:

Evelyn Waugh, Graham Greene, Muriel Spark, Dorothy Sayers, Ronald Knox, Edith Sitwell, Christopher Dawson, Maurice Baring, Arnold Lunn, Malcolm Muggeridge. In these examples and others like them among ordinary people, we should note that the conversions of which we speak include the serious intent to embrace the world's most demanding and lofty moral code. These men and women were by no means looking for an easier and lax morality acceptable to the worldly world. That would be regression, not improvement.

A Word about Motivation

What prompts people to move from mediocrity (or worse) toward a radical reversal to the morally good and the best? Supposing, of course, the illuminating grace of God (available to anyone who really and honestly wants it), evidence indicates that there are almost numberless reasons why serious persons move toward the Church Jesus founded. He surely is the most powerful of them all. Despite the faults of individual members who fail to live up to what they profess, thoughtful people recognize that the only fair way to judge any institution is according to its principles and the example of those who live in accord with them. That simple fact points to the sheer goodness and beauty of the saints, those who live heroically well what Catholicism is and teaches. Where else can we find women like Catherine of Siena, Teresa of Avila, Thérèse of Lisieux and Elizabeth Ann Seton, or men to compare with Augustine, Thomas Aquinas, Francis Xavier and Francis of Assisi, John of the Cross, Thomas More and John Vianney? Only truth can produce these heroes and heroines with their burning love, radiant chastity, overflowing generosity, exquisite patience and fortitude, all that is lofty and noble. They are prime illustrations of the evidential power of beauty. We have pointed out elsewhere and at length that science and theology now converge in their agreement that beauty is the best pointer to truth—whether the matter be an equation of physics, a given lifestyle or a doctrine in theology. (See EPB, especially Chapter 6).

A third motive prompting conversion for many lies in the simple facts of history. Jesus founded only one Church and to her alone he committed his authority and promises: "As the Father has sent me, so I send you . . . He who hears you, hears me; he who rejects you, rejects me . . . I am with you all days even to the end of time" (Jn 20:21; Lk 10:16; Mt 28:20). This is bedrock evidence convincingly rooted in Sacred Scripture and the twenty centuries following Jesus' birth.

Another dimension of history is the fourth reason for many conversions. Jesus' Church teaches everything that he taught with no omissions or alterations to suit the moods of differing times and places. No cafeteria picking and choosing. Unfortunately all groups who through the centuries have left this *ecclesia*, while they retain some doctrines and moral precepts, have left others aside. People like Newman who study ecclesiastical history are aware of this symphony of beauty. They are struck with the wholeness, the unity and the inner radiance of divine revelation as it is preserved in the magisterial office established by Jesus himself. Honest intellectuals seem especially attracted to the coherence, completeness and consistency of this otherworldly phenomenon.

We will content ourselves with one further example of a motivation that underlies many conversions: the shortness of life and the endless duration of eternity, along with the momentous implications of the eternal enthrallment of heaven or the eternal disaster of hell. Jesus put it perfectly: "What does it profit a man to gain the whole world and suffer the loss of his soul?" (Mt 16:26). As sensible people grow older, they see more and more clearly that alienation from God together with the tinsel of worldliness is futility and frustration in this life, and, unless there is repentance, calamity in the next. They are then more inclined to do something about it.

Yet, in my work over several decades, I have on occasion had the happiness to deal in spiritual direction with teenagers and young adults in their twenties who have responded generously and beautifully to divine grace. They have been touched by the Lord and have said a youthful and enthusiastic Yes. Imitating young saints like Agatha, Maria Goretti and Aloysius, these young people come to see what their elders often fail to grasp. They are doubly blessed.

Since we vary a great deal in the depths or shallowness of determination with which we direct our lives and make our commitments and decisions, we turn our attention at this point to the basic and pervasive condition of growth in personal excellence, a deepening moral and prayerful conversion, all the way from the dawn of reason to our final breath.

2

THE RADICAL CONVERSION

God does nothing by happenstance. For him everything has point and purpose. He does not speculate. He knows. He is fully aware of what he is about, and he intends it with complete thoroughness.

We therefore pursue our inquiry into the whats, whys and hows of conversion, in the very way Jesus began speaking publicly about you and me and our destiny. It has to be hugely significant that the first recorded words in his official ministry—indeed, only six words—concerned conversion, the theme of this book. For most of us that would be the last thing we would expect from a stranger speaking to us for the first time. Deep, personal, radical change: "Be converted", he proclaimed to the crowd, "and accept the gospel" (Mk 1:15). Six words, ten syllables!

After twenty centuries of commentary by saints and scholars, it is still safe to say that we still have not fully plumbed the depths of that short sentence. Yet upon analysis we find it brilliant.

Be converted: that is, be changed, refashioned, even transformed from your present condition or stance to another, perhaps an opposite other. That is rather an abrupt way to begin a conversation or a lecture. Jesus did have the habit of surprising people, of saying what no one would expect him to say. Yet I have just remarked that these six words are brilliant. What do I mean?

In my youth I would have expected that, if someone wanted to begin this sort of conversation so suddenly, he would have said something like: accept the gospel and it will convert you. There is truth in this version, of course, but there is a still deeper truth in what Jesus actually did say.

First, a bit of background. Perhaps the most all-embracing trait of the original wound you and I have suffered from our first parents is an omnipresent egocentrism. We experience this I-centeredness every day until hopefully we come closer to saintliness in our lives. Before that blessed time arrives, each of us must admit: Yes, my thoughts and desires and inclinations are spontaneously focused not on others but on myself: my conveniences, my pleasures, my preferences, my possessions, my prospects, my plans, my sufferings, my desires, my aspirations, my reputation, my freedom. Anyone who reflects a bit, who is honest, knows that this is true.

The fundamental conversion is therefore the renouncing of this pervasive egoism and the turning to an altruistic love for objective truth, goodness and beauty. This change is a momentous reversal. It is a switch from a subjective selfishness to seeing and pursuing reality as it objectively is. Growing in this fashion sounds easy only to a superficial person. It is a lifetime task and can happen only with the grace of God and a persevering determination on our part. What this program entails we will discuss in Chapters 8 and 9.

But for now we need to emphasize how tenaciously, even stubbornly, many people cling to the preferences and sympathies of their own way of life even in the face of strong evidences against these preferences. Elemental truths, the way things actually are, leave little impact on most persons' consciousness and routine decisions. This is especially the case with moral and ultimate realities. People love their desires. Newman made this point in his usual penetrating manner, but other careful observers have also noted the following common assumptions of egocentrism: "I am right because this is my preference. I need not consider your reasons and arguments seriously." This is why many married couples (say the experts) argue and fight over and over again about the same disagreements and often with no happy solutions and healing. Egocentrism is probably the main root of human conflicts. Hence, Jesus is saying "love truth, the way things objectively are; do not cling to your preferences when they clash with reality."

Next, he is saying that conversion implies not only loving truth but also goodness: humility, honesty, patience, temperance, fortitude, chastity and all the virtues, most especially genuine love. When we come to love objective truth and goodness, we have made progress toward conversion from our radical "I-ism". This fundamental transformation is completed with the love of beauty, first the beauty of God, and then the beauty of man and the rest of creation. Altruism and egocentrism are opposites.

Now we are prepared to look into the last four words of Jesus' first message to his people ". . . and accept the gospel." How does this follow from the first two words: Be converted? When honest men love objective reality, the way things actually are, and then go on to pursue the goodness of all the virtues and are sensitive to genuine beauty, they are like a starving man sitting before a banquet. He immediately sees the answers to his needs. When people who love truth, goodness and beauty hear the gospel, they spontaneously love it. This means of course that they immediately see its attractiveness and splendor, how it magnificently fulfills their human aspirations and needs. Because they are freed from I-centeredness, they are finely tuned to be receptive of reality, including divine Reality. An honest study of atheism and comparative religion makes it lucidly clear that no other worldview begins to compare with the truth-reality, the sheer beauty and holiness, the incomparable splendor of Jesus and his message throughout the Gospels. Indeed, beauty is evidence of truth.

Artistry and Artists

Art always demands an artist. Always, not merely sometimes. When anthropologists discover a reindeer sketched on the wall of an ancient cave, they are immediately certain that this picture was not drawn by a fellow reindeer. They have not the least doubt that an intellectual being, a person, had to be the artist. As we have noted, the parable of the prodigal son, a work of consummate literary brilliance and divine tenderness, has no equal in all of human literature. It had to come from the mind and heart of a divine artist. When a person is purified of selfishness, he immediately sees the splendor of this parable and much else in the New Testament. Because he is converted to the love of truth, goodness and beauty, he is instantly attracted to embrace the good news.

For sheer surprise, penetration and magnificence our six-word statement about our radical human situation and what to do about it likewise has no equal in secular literature or in other religions. But these traits are found repeatedly in the Gospel accounts of Jesus. As a shortcut to seeing this point, I may refer the reader to G. K. Chesterton's *Everlasting Man*, part 2, chapters 2 and 3. We find there a brilliant discussion of Jesus' unparalleled gifts of brevity, profundity and literary excellence found nowhere else. I might also suggest the view of Feodor Dostoyevsky, who is widely considered the best novelist of the nineteenth century. In one of his letters we read: "I believe there is no one deeper, lovelier, more sympathetic and more perfect than Jesus—not only is there no one else like him, there never could be anyone like him." Not surprisingly in the Lord's own lifetime ordinary people had already come to the same conclusion. Eyewitnesses were amazed at the "gracious words that came from his lips . . . Where did the man get this wisdom?" they wondered (Lk 4:22; Mt 4:28; 13:54). After his teaching on the use of material goods they were more astonished than ever" (Mk 10:26). He repeatedly delighted his listeners with unheard of remarks. Jesus' observations were new, simple and yet so profound that, after twenty centuries, scholars are still finding fresh insights in them. No wonder then that "the people as a whole hung on his words" (Lk 19:48). Their conclusions matched the judgments of Chesterton and Dostoyevsky: indeed no man has ever spoken as this man has. The reason is of course that he happens also to be divine. People who are well on the way to a deep love for truth, goodness and beauty readily embrace his person and his message. Because they are converted, they welcome the gospel —just as Jesus had said they would.

The Offspring of Egocentrism

There are two roots of conflicts in human communities in which people live closely on a daily basis. One is a lack of shared vision regarding the basic principles undergirding our destiny and inter-relationships. This is why Jesus said that a city or household divided into factions cannot last for long (Mt 12:25). The second root of discord is our present concern: egocentrism in its innumerable forms. Even if husbands and wives were to agree about basic principles in their vocation, if they lack a radical conversion from I-centeredness to a generous concern for others, there should be no wonder that conflicts with untold sufferings, major and minor, are a sure result.

While it is true that every sin is a manifestation of this primal woundedness, some illustrations may be of help in finding what needs healing in each of us. A common type of egocentrism is self-indulgent comfort-seeking and unvarnished laziness. A husband may reason that after supper he need not help his wife with washing up the dishes and preparing the youngsters for bedtime: "After all I have had a hard day at the shop or office. I am tired." These two statements may well be true, but how much thought does he give to his spouse's day and how weary she may be? This self-centered indolence can show up also in a religious community. While there are generous members who volunteer far beyond their fair share for everyday menial tasks, there are others who rarely even empty the dishwasher. C. S. Lewis, speaking of an ordinary family, was on target when he remarked, "There cannot be a common life without a *regula* [rule]. The alternative to rule is not freedom but the unconstitutional (and often unconscious) tyranny of the most selfish member" (*God in the Dock*, p. 286). This tyranny may be petty, but it is real among people who are not deeply converted.

I-ism turns up frequently in dishonest speech. Exaggerations, caricatures, even plain lies occur to enhance the vanity and self-image of the conversationalist. Domination in a meeting or in ordinary chatting can serve the same purpose:

my experiences, my stories, my ideas, are more interesting and important than yours, and so it is right that I go on at length, perhaps even interrupting what you have to contribute.

Lust is so obviously egocentric that little needs to be said. Yet in the worldly world "affairs" and the exploitation of another person are often called making love. The playboy type says in action, "I want you not for your sake but for my pleasure—even though I reduce you to the level of a mere toy, a thing, an object. And when I get tired of you, begone . . . I'll exploit and degrade someone else."

Less obvious self-centeredness is found in people who habitually come late and keep others waiting. It can become so frequent in these people that they seem to think it normal. The implication seems clearly to be: "What you have to do is not as important as what I have to do, and so there is no problem in my keeping you waiting for me. My convenience is, after all, paramount." All of which translates into the judgment, "I am more important than you are."

Dozens of other examples could be cited. But we may wrap up our point with one that is both obvious and yet so prevalent that it has become in wealthy societies a major health problem: overeating as regards both quantity and types of food. Lack of temperance in all of its specific forms openly contradicts an objective love for truth, goodness and beauty. This is the case not only in the moral/spiritual realm but also increasingly in current medical literature. Saint Paul put the matter perfectly twenty centuries ago: "Whether you eat or drink or do anything else, do all for the glory of God" (1 Cor 10:31). And God's glory is the same thing as our human good. As Saint Irenaeus put it about eighteen centuries ago: "A man alive is a glory to God."

We have in this chapter an example of what Hans Urs von Balthasar expresses as a three-word gem: "Truth is symphonic". An orchestra performing a Mozart masterpiece provides an experience of delightful beauty to the extent that the conductor and each of the musicians is following the original score. If one of the latter dissents from the mind and text of the maestro because "I know better and so I will go my own way", he can distort a thing of beauty into chaotic ugliness. What is true of music is also true of morality and theology. Truth is indeed symphonic.

This is another way of explaining why the saints are the most beautiful persons in the world. They live the symphony of divine revelation not only well, but heroically well. They are therefore ideal illustrations of the point we are making: loving objective truth, goodness and beauty, rather than our own wounded selfishnesses, prompts a love for the gospel and for the Lord of the gospel.

When this symphony of splendor is lived to the hilt, as our canonized saints have lived it, we find perfect human beauty: deep conversion/deep love. Which was magnificently said approximately twenty-five centuries ago: "You were renowned among the nations for your beauty, perfect as it was, because of my splendor, which I had bestowed on you, says the Lord God" (Ezek 16:14). Our point cannot be made more elegantly.

3

DEGREES OF DEPTH

Genuine love is never static; it grows steadily even if imperceptibly. So also with conversion from bad to good, good to better and better to best. Once a person has undergone the radical change from an egocentric fixation to an objective love of truth, goodness and beauty, progress should be resolute even if gradual. We come therefore to explain the main outlines of what deepening conversion looks like in actual life.

For the purpose of clarity we will distinguish three main degrees of human excellences, natural and supernatural, even though they do occur in numberless shades of perfection. There is the fundamental or basic degree, then the advancing and finally the consummate. We readily see these three stages in singing, ice skating, cooking, teaching and so on. In the moral order we can speak of the basic conversion as a freedom from mortal sins. The advancing level is the giving up of willed venial sins. The consummate or perfect level is the totality of heroic goodness, going all the way with God, loving without limits.

The First Degree of Moral Conversion

We need to ask first of all: what is a mortal sin? It is the knowing, free and willing rejection of God in favor of choosing something incompatible with him. This alienation from him is not a mere mistake but rather a knowing choice that includes preferring some created idol that excludes loving him and our neighbor. A mortal, deadly sin is a freely chosen rejection of supreme Beauty and Goodness, the blessed Trinity. Examples include torture, murder, adultery, blasphemy, hatred, lust, gross injustices. As Jesus put it: we cannot have God and mammon, that is, things not God, idols (Mt 6:24). This rejection, if unrepented, leads to freely chosen eternal disaster. Those who end up in hell have themselves knowingly chosen to reject God forever. The Lord, the very fullness of tender mercy, forces himself on no one.

The first degree of conversion, therefore, is a 180-degree reversal: "I renounce my idol, Lord; I want you instead. I am sorry, very sorry. With your grace I am going to change my life. I freely choose to repent. I shall receive your sacrament of reconciliation." The perfect portrayal of this basic conversion is found in Jesus' parable of the prodigal son (Lk 15:11–32). The fundamental friendship with God is restored. (See also Chapter Ten).

The Second Degree

The second stage of conversion builds on the first, for much remains to be done. Here the person makes efforts to avoid small wrongs, venial sins. These do not destroy one's essential love for God and neighbor, but they do wound it. Even though they are not colossal, they remain disorders. They cool but do not extinguish the love relationship with God and our neighbor. Ordinary gossiping and overeating are examples. The reader should notice that when we speak above about "willed venial sins" the first adjective is important indeed. Without intellectual awareness and, therefore, freedom there is no willing, no sin. We are talking about things we can control, not mere mistakes, not mere feelings, which to a large extent we cannot control. For example, it is not a sin to feel impatient when children or adults annoy us by obnoxious behavior, especially when it is repeated or persistent. Sin here means guilt. There is no guilt, thus no sin unless we freely choose some wrong action or omission. To snap back at a person usually is a free action and thus with guilt. We ordinarily can control what we say. If one has the habit of snapping when annoyed, he ought to work at getting rid of the habit. Another example: it is not a sin to feel grouchy, but it can be a sin to be grouchy—after all, while we cannot fully control how we feel, we can make an effort to be pleasant even on a hard day. A third example: an unchaste thought flitting through one's mind, but with no will behind it, is not guilt laden, not a sin. Hence the second degree of conversion occurs when a person no longer willingly and deliberately clings to minor faults. Yes, there may be the occasional slip through half advertence or a momentary weakness, but in that case there is genuine repentance and serious effort to avoid the slip in the future.

The Third and Highest Degree

As we have noted above, there are several ways of describing this third step of conversion: loving God and neighbor without limit, giving oneself beyond the call of duty, going all the way with God, living like the saints lived. Chesterton called this lofty holiness a revolution. At this stage of growth these individuals are not simply rather better than ordinarily good folk—they are vastly superior in sheer goodness.

Sacred Scripture and the liturgy (which is largely made

up of biblical passages and allusions to the divine word) frequently call us to this heroic holiness. For example, we are to be perfect as our heavenly Father is perfect . . . to be holy as he is holy . . . to be as pure as Christ . . . to be holy and blameless living through love in the divine presence . . . to be fully developed as persons with nothing missing (Mt 5:48; 1 Pet 1:15; 1 Jn 3:3; Eph 1:4; Jas 1:4).

We hear and read admonitions to lofty sanctity so often from Saint Paul and other saints that we often fail to notice how sublime they are. Paul never says simply "be rather filled with the Holy Spirit"—85 percent is not enough, nor is 98 percent. Rather what he does insist on is "Be filled with the Spirit", that is without limit (Eph 5:18).

Illustrations: Scripture, Liturgy, Saints

Anyone who reads the biblical message attentively, participates devoutly in the Mass and the Liturgy of the Hours and reads lives of the saints with some frequency will readily recall how replete these sources are with examples and calls to the heights. The fact that the teaching Church provides and recommends these three radical sources of the divine message to everyone in each state in life is an eloquent statement in practice that we are all of us called to saintliness, not to something less. This is not the place to present a multitude of examples, for they abound in the sources we have just mentioned. Hence, we will be brief.

First, the New Testament. In Hebrews 10:34 we read of the faithful who for the truth have suffered the griefs and miseries of first century prisons, that they "happily accepted being stripped of [their] belongings, knowing that [they] owned something that was better and lasting" (JB). Three details should be carefully noticed and weighed in that sentence about astonishing holiness. These people are stripped of their belongings, everything is gone: furniture, beds, carpets, lamps, clothing, keepsakes, decorations, food and all else. . . . The house itself is stolen or destroyed. Most people would consider all this a disaster. Next we observe the adverb, "happily" accepted. Imagine a twenty-first-century couple, who, upon returning from a month of business or vacation and finding that their car and home with everything in it has been destroyed or stolen by a persecuting government, exclaim to each other "darling, isn't this marvelous?" as they embrace in mutual delight. Last, we notice the motive. This couple are not pagans or spartans. They are christic people, disciples of Jesus with their hearts set not on this world of time, but on the enthrallment to which they are destined—the beatific vision in risen body. This sublime sanctity is not of this world; it has a divine stamp on it.

For a sampling from our Catholic liturgy we may take almost at random one day from our 365 (or 366) celebrations each year: Friday of the third week of Lent. In the opening prayer we pray, "Merciful Father, fill our hearts with your love . . ." If a person is filled with love, not something less, that person is heroically holy. The couple we have just considered could not have reacted to their disaster in the way they did, except that they were already loving God totally and were thus transformed in his awesome power (as Saint John of the Cross explains). Further on, in the responsorial Psalm 81, we read that the Lord wishes to feed us "with the best of wheat, and with honey from the rock I would fill them." In this metaphorical and poetic language God is telling all of us that he wishes to bring us to the loftiest and most beautiful fulfillment, but that he will not force it upon us: "I would like to fill them . . ." In the Gospel reading for this liturgy (Mk 12:28-34) we hear the greatest among the commandments, that we love the Lord our God with all our heart, soul, mind and strength, and our neighbor as ourselves. That means that there remains no least trace of selfishness, egocentrism. The person is living a life of love pure and simple (2 Jn 6). Or as Saint John of the Cross charmingly describes a person in the transforming union: walking lovesick for God. Once again this sanctity is not of this world; it has the divine handwriting all over it. Our final examples in this Lenten liturgy occur in the closing prayer, which not only repeats the petition that the "Lord fill us with the power of his love", but that we may "come to know [experience] fully the redemption we have received." When a person experiences God fully on earth, he is at the pinnacle of intimacy with the indwelling Trinity, the transforming union.

We may illustrate heroic virtue in the saints with a statement from the master of the loftiest prayer. Saint John of the Cross uses the sevenfold imagery of Saint Teresa's mansions to explain how there is not the least doubt that, if a person is faithful to grace at whatever stage of growth he may be, he will most surely eventually reach the very peak of moral goodness and contemplative intimacy with the Trinity:

> If a man remains faithful . . . the Lord will not cease raising him degree by degree until he reaches the divine union and transformation. . . . If the individual is victorious over the devil in the first degree, he will pass on to the second; and if so in the second, he will go to the third; and likewise through all the seven mansions. (AMC, bk. 2, chap. 11, no. 9).

In one of his homilies Saint Bernard graphically makes the same point. Speaking of the loftiest contemplative prayer, the saint declares to the sinner that no matter into what slime of sin he has descended in the past, he is still called to the very heights of prayer. The sinner's part in complete conversion is fidelity to the graces he is given at each point of his ascent out of the pit. A marvel of divine tenderness and power!

Many of us have read of how Saint Maximilian Kolbe, priest and religious, practiced heroic love for God and neighbor when in a Nazi prison he offered himself for martyrdom in the place of the condemned father of a family. All through the centuries we have other astonishing spectacles of endless streams of splendid men and women being tortured to death loving and praying for their persecutors, all in fidelity to truth and goodness. These glories of Catholicism have their successors today as people still suffer in the brutal regimes found in our contemporary world.

Then there is what we might term the white martyrdom of a man like Saint John Vianney, the Curé of Ars. He lived the martyr's total love for God and neighbor when for decades on end, and with no vacation, he would spend from ten to eighteen hours night and day in a tiny confessional box continuously listening to tales of woe, advising and healing thousands of sin-laden penitents. This grinding, love-motivated crucifixion he would begin at one o'clock in the morning and, with some interruptions from his other priestly duties, on into late evening. People had to wait up to seven days for the privilege of being healed in this sacrament by this hero of brotherly love—all triggered by the saint's inner fire of divine love. This is what heroic goodness looks like in a real human life.

Hundreds, thousands of scholarly, well-documented accounts like our above examples can be found in any reasonably complete Catholic library.

The Summit: A Still Closer Look

Our discussion of deep conversion needs still further analysis, even in this admittedly summary account. In the eighteenth century Benedict XIV, a brilliant theologian even before he was elected to the papal office, wrote a four-volume study *The Beatification and Canonization of the Servants of God*, a work still of value today in determining heroic virtues in beatification and canonization processes. (See NCE, s.v. "Benedict XIV, Pope", M. L. Shay, 2:278; s.v. "Virtue, heroic", K. V. Truhlar, 14:709–10.) While we cannot hope in this limited space to give an adequate account of the richness of our subject, a brief sketch is preferable to nothing at all.

We can speak of conversion not only as avoiding sins, mortal and venial, but also positively, as changes, improvements from evil to good: from lying to honesty . . . vanity to humility . . . gluttony to temperance . . . foolishness to prudence . . . timidity to courage . . . rage to patience . . . laziness to zeal . . . lust to love . . . cheating to justice . . . pettiness (small mindedness) to magnanimity (large mindedness) . . . egoism to altruism . . . mediocrity to totality . . . personal ugliness to personal beauty. Heroism in holiness occurs, wrote Benedict XIV, when these and the other virtues attain that peak of perfection by which a person vastly surpasses the goodness of ordinarily faithful people who aspire to holiness but at a slower pace and with less effort.

Heroic virtues are also interconnected. A person does not simply have one or a few virtues to a splendid degree. All the perfect virtues are found together. If an individual grows only in one or a few virtues, but lacks others, he is either a beginner or is becoming lax. Saint Francis de Sales is strong and clear. In speaking of the four cardinal virtues he writes that "Justice is not justice unless it be strong, prudent and temperate; nor is prudence prudence unless it be temperate, just and strong; nor fortitude fortitude unless it be just, prudent and temperate; nor temperance temperance unless it be prudent, strong and just" (TLG, bk. 11, c. 7).

In the state of perfection the sundry virtues are connected also with fidelity to and perseverance in one's duties of state in life: marriage, consecrated life, priesthood. Therefore the saintly person need not do extraordinary or unusual things (unless circumstances may on occasion call for such), but he must be devoted to the daily nitty-gritty of his vocation. And, of course, every state in life calls for fidelity to prayer and growing intimacy with the Trinity.

We may point out several general traits of people who have grown to this level of holiness. They stand out from common folk in a number of ways we may distinguish.

1. Their acts of the given virtue are numerous and habitual. They are patient and humble and cheerful and gentle not only once in a while when they feel so disposed, but whenever circumstances call for that particular goodness.

2. Not only is the perfection of the particular action present in each case, but the intensity of the love which prompts it is greater than in the case of most sincere people. If through semi-advertence or surprise or momentary weakness there is on some occasion a venial fault, it is much regretted and carefully avoided in the future.

3. These people are prompt in what needs to be done. They do not delay or procrastinate. Saint Luke notes in his Gospel that when the Mother of Jesus learned that her cousin Elizabeth needed help, she went in haste into the hill country to provide that service (Lk 1:39). Saint Ambrose comments on this verse that the grace of the Holy Spirit knows no delay.

4. The saintly person seems to find it easy to live on this level not only in daily routines but even in painful and difficult situations—as, for example, being gentle in nursing an obnoxious patient, or in suffering oneself in a trying illness, or while being tortured in martyrdom. We should notice that our expression "seems to find it easy" does not mean that these heroic people do not experience piercing pain. They suffer as all the rest of us do. But the difference is, as Saint John of the Cross noted, they possess an "awesome strength" in the transforming union, a strength that shares in divine power, so close is their intimacy with the indwelling Trinity. While Saint Thomas More was in prison awaiting a gruesome execution, a visitor asked him how he felt. He answered that he felt like a school boy on a holiday.

5. Heroic holiness is lived in cheerful joy. Martyrs are known to have faced their tortures singing and praising God, loving and praying for their tormenters. Saint Paul says of the first-century faithful, "You will have in you the strength, based on his own glorious power, never to give in, but to bear anything joyfully, thanking the Father . . ." (Col 1:11 JB). "To bear *anything* joyfully, thanking the Father . . . !" It is easy to see in this one verse how and why the saints are moral miracles: their goodness and beauty far surpass the natural capacities of human nature. Anyone who doubts this fact, either does not know himself, or he refuses to see what is as obvious as the nose on his face.

6. As I have pointed out elsewhere, "heroically holy people unite in themselves virtues that seem to many people to exclude one another: magnanimity (aspiring to do great things for God and our neighbor) and humility, warm love and chastity, contemplation and action. Chinese intellectual John Wu was struck especially with this trait in Saint Thérèse of Lisieux, and he was moved to enter the Catholic Church

because he saw that these highly desirable qualities cannot result from mere human ingenuity and strength. Wu concluded that the Church that could produce a Thérèse has to be his home of the divine on earth, for he found in this young woman 'a living synthesis of such opposite extremes as humility and boldness, freedom and discipline, joy and suffering, duty and love, strength and tenderness, grace and nature, wisdom and folly, wealth and poverty, community and individualism.' " (Guy Gaucher, *Sainte Thérèse de Lisieux aux extremities du monde*, p. 25 in EPB, p. 252).

Since each of the divine commandments spells out what is good for the individual and for all of us in our various states in life, a person who carries them out is bound to be a beautiful human being. And since each precept also indicates what love requires in a given set of circumstances, the individual with heroic virtues is doing exactly what Scripture indicates: "living a life of love" (2 Jn 6.).

We readily see upon these few reflections why Pope John Paul II was entirely right in his prayer for the Jubilee Year of 2000. At the outset of it, after praising the Trinity, his very first petition in the name of the universal Church was: "By your grace, O Father, may the Jubilee Year be a time of deep conversion and of joyful return to you." Perfectly on target.

4

CALL TO THE HEIGHTS

We need to address at this point a strange situation. Intelligent and sincere people often have a great difficulty in giving what John Henry Newman called a real assent to what we have already noted in the Gospel about the call to saintliness. They may well intellectually agree (notional assent was Newman's term) with everything we have so far noted, for after all the divine message could hardly be more explicit. But that this message is addressed to every married man and woman, every priest and bishop, every farmer and laborer, every politician and cab driver, every student, and especially addressed to you the reader and to me the writer, that at least takes some getting used to.

Hence a closer look is in order. A real assent to a proposition includes the intellectual acceptance of it plus the concrete carrying out of it in the nitty-gritty of daily life, that is, making this truth part of one's personal reality. This specific problem we will address in our next chapter. For the moment we now consider sharpening up our mind's grasp and conviction about saintliness, not something less. Yes, the heights of holiness are for you and me, period. No matter what our past may have been, no matter how far we may be from the summit right now, no matter what state in life or career we are in, no matter what temperament or inclinations we have, no matter what our job may be, we are called to be saints.

God pays every one of us the huge compliment of calling us to the personal excellence of magnificent goodness: heroic love, humility, fortitude, patience, chastity, honesty and all the virtues without exception. Scripture takes this for granted over and over again and never tires of explicitly proclaiming it: We are to be perfect as God himself is perfect . . . We are to be transformed from one glory to another into the very divine image . . . We should be so intimate with the indwelling Trinity that we live a life of love: everything we do becomes an act of loving . . . We cannot even imagine what splendors await us if we actually love God and neighbor as we ought . . . We are not only to be possessed by the Holy Spirit, but to be filled with him—yes, filled . . . We are to desire the Lord with all of our strength, not just a high degree of it . . . In one verse Jesus insists four times that we are to love this God of ours with a whole heart, whole soul, whole mind and all of our strength . . . Thus the faithful in all states of life are to become marvelously beautiful, famous among the nations for their beauty, perfect in this splendor—all because the Lord bestows it on those who decide to seek him fully (Mt 5:48; 2 Cor 3:18; 2 Jn 6; 1 Cor 2:9; Eph 5:18; Ps 119:10; Lk 10:27; Ezek 16:13–14). If the reader wishes a book-length explanation of this heroic holiness and deepest intimacy with the Trinity, see the author's *Fire Within*.

Everyone who attends Mass regularly should easily recognize that these biblical texts and others like them are heard over and over again in the course of the liturgical year. Hence the teaching Church is saying that they are meant for everyone. All of us without exception are to take them seriously. In each of these texts the Church is affirming that all of her children are called to be saints, profoundly converted to the highest degree of sanctity. No other worldview presents and proclaims so beautiful and lofty an ideal of what man can become—indeed should become. One may look into Buddhist, Hindu, Islamic writings to verify what we are saying here. Needless to say, atheistic and merely secular literature does not bear even a faint resemblance to this heroic grandeur and beauty.

Moreover, Vatican Council II was at pains to devote an entire chapter in its *Constitution on the Church* to this good news of great joy. Chapter 5, "The Call to Holiness", after laying down the principle that everyone in the Church is called to holiness, then goes on to apply this to each group of the faithful. Bishops, priests, deacons and the ministers of lesser rank are to give themselves to "an outstanding example of holiness" in their prayer lives and in sacrificing themselves fully for the benefit of all the flock. Husbands and wives are to support each other in their faithful love, and form their children with revealed truth in the practice of all the virtues. In this they witness to the motherhood of the Church in her fruitfulness. Widows and single people are also to contribute to the sanctity and activity of the Church, as are workers of all types. Those experiencing illness, poverty and all sorts of suffering are to imitate Jesus who was tortured to death for the love of his brothers, each one of us. Martyrs who so closely imitate the Lord on his Cross give the greatest testimony of their heroic love for all, even for their persecutors. They teach all of us how to bear persecution for the truth, whether it is at the hands of terrorists or in the injustices the genuine followers of Jesus must bear in secularized societies and sometimes because of the media (see LG, nos. 39–42).

Because the Master in his own person gave the perfect

example of total devotion to the Father with an undivided heart in virginity and poverty, Vatican Council II focused a special attention on the men and women in the Church who embrace consecrated life. Through their vows of celibacy, poverty and obedience they imitate him who was chaste, who became poor for our sakes and who was obedient unto death (2 Cor 8:9; Phil 2:7–8). In these three radical renunciations (all aimed at total love) these dedicated ones remind the world at large of the beauty of chastity in every state in life . . . and of the spirit and fact of evangelical frugality which all the faithful are called to follow in their use of material goods. (See no. 42 in LG, and for a fuller explanation one may consult the author's *Happy Are You Poor*).

In the twenty centuries of the Church's history there is no ecumenical council that so frequently and so eloquently spoke of contemplative intimacy with the indwelling Trinity as did this last council. Approximately eighty times Vatican II dealt with deep prayer, often using the word contemplation to express this intimacy.

We here mention just one of these fourscore references. In the *Constitution on the Sacred Liturgy*, number 10, the Council discusses the profound participation of the faithful in the celebration of Mass. This passage reminds us that during the offering the Eucharistic liturgy all of us are to taste, to experience fully—not something less—of this paschal mystery. Indeed, this renewal of the Lord's covenant in Mass draws the faithful into a compelling love "and sets them afire". This burning love reminds us of Psalm 34:8 where we read of tasting and drinking deeply of the goodness of the Lord. When a person reaches this depth he is close to the pinnacle of holiness.

We are now prepared to tackle the practical problems of

growing in personal excellence. And first of all we must face honestly and deal adequately with a surprise, a huge surprise for those who are less than saints. The problems can be formidable, but they do have solutions.

5

A REMARKABLE RESISTANCE

We now turn our attention to a phenomenon that is both common and extraordinary—from two different points of view, of course. Let me explain.

Most of us would like to assume that when reasonable people hear about improving themselves notably in their personal lives they would more or less eagerly welcome the message and get to work applying it. We would like to think that a husband and father who claims that he loves his wife and children will prove it in the minor details of daily life as well as in the major ones. And we entertain a similar expectation of a wife and mother who makes the same claim. We may sharpen our point still more keenly. Normal people would tend to suppose that if a person basically loves God, is living in the state of grace and is therefore free from a serious alienation from God, his Origin and Destiny, he would be strongly committed to avoiding small offenses against this most magnificent of all loves.

But the rude fact is that such consistency in the human race is rather rare. A few moments of careful reflection makes that clear. Petty gossiping, lies, laziness, vanities seem to worry many people very little—at least not enough to spark significant changes. Something is radically wrong, amiss, out of kilter—or as a laborer might express it, something is basically out of whack. We consider ourselves to be rational beings, but those of us less than saints commonly act irrationally in these areas of life. Egoisms, even petty egoisms, make no sense. Yet they are common. How do we explain this pathetic situation?

The only sensible explanation that I have ever come across is our theological development of the ancient doctrine of original sin. If the reader is a theologian, he should know the voluminous literature where this is competently and solidly treated. If one is interested in a less complicated discussion, he can find it in the *Catechism of the Catholic Church*, nos. 388–421. This whole volume on deep conversion/deep prayer is a practical path pointing the way out of this wretched plight. We are always, of course, supposing the grace won for us by Jesus on his Cross and in his Resurrection. We are not Pelagians; we cannot lift ourselves out of a deadening mediocrity by our bootstraps.

Our immediate purpose at this point is to focus on the remarkable resistance most people place before significant moral change happening in their lives. We may begin our analysis by recalling what we said at the outset of Chapter 1 about Saint Bernard of Clairvaux and his arresting statement to the effect that there are more people converted from mortal sin to grace than there are people converted from good to better . . . and, we added, to best.

The main thrust of this book is *deep* conversion. It is a subject seldom talked about, even thought about. Few of us recall ever hearing a lecture, indeed, a ten-minute homily on the theme. For most people it simply is not an issue. To his great credit Bernard faced it head on and spoke the plain truth that every one of us lesser mortals should face honestly—if we are determined to get out of the pervasive rut of mediocrity.

I would not want to guess how many in our human family live in the state of serious alienation from God, that is, in mortal, deadly sin. God knows this and I do not. I am now wondering how it happens that theists, not simply worldly materialists, more commonly give up their mortal sins than give up lesser ones. I am thinking especially of those who come into weekly, even daily contact with biblical and liturgical readings. They know of our breathtakingly beautiful christic revelation. They have heard probably dozens of times of many of the texts and ideas in our previous chapter on the universal call to the heights of inner beauty and happiness. Most of these theists have heard or read more or less of the saints, those heroes and heroines of sanctity in all states of life. How does it happen, we are asking, that comparatively few of these people give up their willed venial sins? Recall that we are not asking about what we cannot control: feelings of impatience or resentment, for example. We are speaking of freely willed actions we can stop if we want to stop. Why do people who love God to some extent knowingly choose not to love him completely? Why do they not give up their petty clingings?

The answer must be the title of this chapter: a remarkable resistance. It is surely no exaggeration to say that if we lived 1 percent of what we hear and see and read in our splendid Catholic liturgies in a year or a month, we would be saints long ago. If anyone is tempted to think this sentence is an overstatement, I am afraid that he has given little thought to the matter. There is a great gap for most people between prayer and performance. At our devotions we can say sublime things about loving God with our whole heart, and then ten minutes later divide that heart with selfish overeating—or any one of a dozen other petty clingings. One who is attentive and thinks it over for just a little while knows this to be true.

This resistance is probably not explicitly perceived. Very few of us sit down one day and say "I do not want to change for the better; I won't get better; I won't even try." More likely than not we may wish we were better. But a wish is a velleity, a mere weak desire that leads nowhere. Unfortunately this remarkable resistance in most people is a fact, an undoubted reality. Let me be specific with examples, then we can examine ourselves honestly. There are people who, in their teens and twenties, gossiped about others' faults, and they are still at it in their thirties and forties and fifties—probably wishing on occasion that they were not doing it. Yet they could stop but they do not. Yes, they continue the habit in their sixties and seventies, with perhaps a choice morsel to tattle on their deathbed. It could well happen that they have confessed this sin in their monthly confessions, but nothing changes much. Possibly the aberration has increased in frequency over the years.

Have these people forgotten what they learned at their mother's knee or in catechism class about a firm purpose of amendment? A firm decision means of course: "I intend to stop this habit. I can stop it if I want to, and I will take means to get over it." Have they really been sorry for these sins when they go to confession? If they have been sorry, really sorry, why has there been little or no change in something concerning which they have free will?

In place of this gossiping example we can insert any number of venial sins: little dishonesties; egocentric conversations; showing impatience; wasting time with television, that is, something not beneficial or useful; slowness in turning away from immodest scenes or pictures; omitting prayer or spiritual reading out of laziness; overeating or eating foods harmful to health; small lies. The reader can probably add to this list of illustrations. It is by no means complete. And it is obvious that these venial sins can also be found throughout the decades of a person's life, a person who basically wants God, but does not love totally. What is to be done about this dismal picture we will take up in Chapter 9.

While we are thinking in a theistic context, it may be well for us to learn more about this basic human woundedness from a completely secular example. In the August 2, 1999, issue of *Newsweek* magazine, there appeared a cover story about how many Americans know what a healthy diet is and how poorly they live what they know is beneficial. As is usually the case with cover stories of this type, the discussion was complete with statistics and poll questions. To get a feel for the results of the poll, we may reflect on a summary paragraph:

> Consider the findings on diet. Though 91 percent of the respondents agree that eating five servings of fruits and vegetables each day is "important to maintaining a healthy lifestyle," more than a third eat just two servings. And while 92 percent believe it takes two servings of milk, yogurt or cheese each day to meet the body's need for calcium, roughly four in 10 eat less than that. Only 13 percent of those polled say they eat six servings of grain each day, even though most think it important. And while 83 percent agree that we should "limit sugar and fatty foods to one serving per day," majorities of both men and women say they exceed that threshold (p. 48).

We should notice that this paragraph is what people say of themselves; it is not what outsiders think, guess, say or write.

The sentence that precedes this cited paragraph brings us exactly to our point: "Worse yet, the poll results suggest that what we know has very little effect on how we live." This statement could be expressed in neon lights, for it says exactly what lies beneath the remarkable resistance we are analyzing in this chapter. "What we know has very little effect on how we live." This applies not only to a wise use of food, but also to what we know from the beautiful moral teachings of Scripture, what we see in the lives of the saints and celebrate in our liturgies all through each year. "What we know has very little effect on how we live."

However, a caution is in order. The general statement should be qualified, for there are people who are growing in deep conversion as they are growing in prayerful intimacy with the Trinity. What these know does influence their daily decisions, but they are not the majority—as we have been saying. To be completely accurate the sentence should read: *for most people* what they know has very little effect on how they live. And here lies the root of our remarkable resistance to getting rid of venial sins and going on to heroic virtue.

Something else should be noted in this analysis of our sad situation. We need to return to Chapter 2, for in the *Newsweek* article we find new reasons to marvel at the profound wisdom contained in the first six words of Jesus' public ministry: "Be converted, and accept the gospel" (Mk 1:15). Whatever else the Lord had in mind with those first two words, he surely meant on the deepest level: "Be rid of your egoism, your self-centeredness. Rather love objective truth, goodness and beauty." What does loving truth mean? As we have already explained, it means loving reality, the way things actually are. Truth is the conformity of the mind with reality. Conversion here entails renouncing one's selfish, egoistic, excessive pleasures and desires in favor of welcoming creation and its beauty, using it as it is meant to be used, and most of all embracing the lovable Creator of it all.

We then apply this to the magazine article: what most people know has very little effect on how they live. The reason obviously is that most love their pleasures in eating and drinking more than they value their real purposes: health and energy for working out our eternal destiny and aiding others to do the same. They do not love objective truth. That is why they go to excess, even in some cases to the point of addiction. They need radical conversion.

Jesus is also brilliantly saying: love goodness, that is, seek and practice all the virtues, and in our example, the virtue of temperance in your use of food and drink. Select what you shall eat and drink in accordance with what is best for your health, not what may flatter your taste buds but damage your well-being and ability to serve others as well. He is saying also: be moderate and realistically motivated. In other words, be converted. Give up your self-centeredness and love truth, goodness and beauty. No matter how far you are advanced or how wayward you are in your spiritual life, if this fundamental change is taking place, you are on your way up, on your way to becoming beautiful. It may take time, but it can happen with the grace of God—which is always present.

Hence, our conclusion is that the remarkable resistance we experience in getting rid of faults that we can control is radically rooted in our desperate need for what this book is all about: deep conversion/deep prayer.

The logical reaction at this point for any sincere reader understandably may be: "Help! I can't do this by myself." And of course, that is perfectly true. The Lord took care of this problem too. Without his Holy Spirit, he told us, we can do nothing (1 Cor 12:3). Surely no one can become a saint without his aid. But the fact is that his help and grace are always present. It is up to us to use what he offers but never forces.

So what can you and I do to cooperate with what God wants to give but will not impose? Right at the moment you are holding the answer in your hands. This book is an attempt to explain systematically and somewhat thoroughly what the Lord has already taught. We have yet much more to say, for it is an immensely rich subject. Later on we shall spell out in detail a practical program, a surefire guide to co-operating with what the Lord wants to give you, how all of this can be worked out with patience and determination. We shall not offer gimmicks or clever psychological tips. They do not and cannot bring about the deep inner and genuine transformation with which we are dealing. This latter sort of transformation is a matter of personal authenticity, not something less.

We therefore proceed to our next logical step, the question of motivation in this whole process of deep conversion and deep intimacy with the Trinity.

6

RELEVANCE AND MOTIVATION

We now tackle a problem which, for not a few of our human family, is not easy to solve. I refer to the difficulty of seeing one's own degree of imperfection in the moral life. It is true that unprincipled, incorrigible people often do not see the degree of their baseness, if indeed they see it at all. Saint Paul remarks that the worldly person "does not accept the things of the Spirit . . . he considers it all as nonsense, something beyond his grasp" (1 Cor 2:14). But this is not our main concern here. Rather we now envision a lack of moral perception in people who would shrink from serious crimes, but do not see anything wrong with idle talk or acting with mixed motivation in lesser matters. If they do recognize something amiss in gossiping about another's fault or in overeating, they make little of it. Hans Urs von Balthasar put it well when he said that "sin obscures sight". This is especially true of things that matter most in human life.

We are dealing here with moral mediocrity—which is an opposite way of addressing the focus of this book, deep conversion. Saint Teresa of Avila once insightfully described the problem in just a few words. Speaking of the morally lukewarm, she remarked that they enjoy their mediocrity. In the center of one of our sizeable cities, I once noticed a bumper sticker on the car in front of me: "I am damn good". We can be sure the owner was not a saint—deeply converted people would be the last to fancy that they have reached a lofty degree of perfection.

Allan Bloom in his best-seller, *The Closing of the American Mind*, wrote about college students as having an acute sense of bodily beauty, but scarcely a clue as to what beauty of the soul might be. This remark may be aimed at many of their elders as well. These facts, and who would seriously contest them, point to a dismal contemporary myopia, if not plain blindness. More recently the immensely popular *National Geographic* magazine featured an article on the human quest for physical comeliness:

> The search for beauty is costly. In the United States last year people spent six billion dollars on fragrance and another six billion on makeup. Hair- and skin-care products drew eight billion dollars each, while fingernail items alone accounted for a billion. In the mania to lose weight 20 billion was spent on diet products and services—in addition to the billions that were paid out for health club memberships and cosmetic surgery (January 2000, p. 105).

That comes to forty-nine billion dollars in a twelve-month period spent on bodies that are soon to age and then disappear. Can one imagine what these huge sums could do for the emaciated bodies of the poorest of the poor still living in Haiti, Calcutta and elsewhere? And who could reckon the millions and millions of hours spent by teenagers and their parents annually in primping up before mirrors in comparison to the paltry amounts of time they spend in prayerful intimacy with the indwelling Trinity? And yet the latter activity produces a beauty that shall endure for an endless eternity, while the former objects of endless efforts will shortly dissolve in their graves.

Yes, von Balthasar hit the nail on the head: sin does obscure sight . . . badly and tragically. This myopia, bordering on blindness, we address in this chapter: the malignant obtuseness of iniquity, the nearsightedness of moral mediocrity. Explaining the relevance of deep conversion to these people in some cases is akin to describing the loveliness of Michelangelo's Pietà to a person blind from birth. Nonetheless, we have no choice but to try and to hope that readers may respond to divine enlightening grace that can make clear what is objectively obvious to anyone who begins to be converted to love truth, goodness and beauty. (See again Mk 1:15.) Understanding myopic mediocrity will likewise cast light on a part of what lies behind the remarkable resistance to deep conversion of which we have spoken in our last chapter. As an introduction to what we now discuss, the reader would do well to ponder the searing indictment of moral lukewarmness we find in the last book of Sacred Scripture. To the community in Sardis is proclaimed a blunt message in no uncertain terms:

> I know all about you: how you are reputed to be alive and yet are dead. Wake up; revive what little you have left: it is dying fast. So far, I have failed to notice anything in the way you live that my God could possibly call perfect, and yet do you remember how eager you were when you first heard the message? Hold on to that. Repent (Rev 3:1-3 JB).

The solution to their dire laxity is repentance, pure and simple . . . another way of speaking of the theme of this volume. But there is more: this same chapter of Revelation includes a lacerating condemnation of moral mediocrity. To the community of Laodicea we read:

> I know all about you; how you are neither cold nor hot. I wish you were one or the other, but since you are neither,

but only lukewarm, I will spit you out of my mouth. You say to yourself, "I am rich, I have made a fortune, and have everything I want," never realizing that you are wretchedly and pitiably poor, and blind and naked too . . . (Rev 3:15–17).

I recommend to the reader to pursue the rest of this indictment (vv. 18–22). Once again the solution is conversion: "Repent in real earnest" (v. 19). The Lord lovingly knocks at their doors, and they can, if they will it, join him in his victory and even share in his throne and that of the Father himself (vv. 20–22). How this victory comes about we begin to discuss in this chapter on motivation. Then we will continue the remedy in following chapters, concluding with our sure-fire program and sacramental healing.

The First Motive for Deep Conversion

So we now ask: What is the relevance of deep conversion, deep repentance? What are the compelling reasons why getting cured of venial sins is so crucial, so essential in your life and in mine? (We are now taking for granted the first degree of conversion, and will explicitly deal with the third later on.) It may be best for us to begin with what is closest to most of us: the family and marriage.

Specialists who deal with the interrelationships between husbands and wives and the problems in their marriages entertain a dim view regarding the conflicts found in the typical home. A recent book, for example, was entitled *Marriage Is Hell*, and in a contemporary article the author declared that "All couples fight. And, research shows, most argue about the same things, over and over again. It's human nature to assume change—on the other person's part, of course—is the solution" (*Newsweek*, March 20, 2000, p. 78).

What to think of these two opinions? Two comments are in order. The first is that, while both are making valid points, as they stand they are false. Marriage is not hell. Nor do all couples fight—many do and a few do not. What is hellish are marriages in which the spouses are not living according to the divine plan, or they are not deeply converted from their sins, mortal and venial. The same is true of faults in the priesthood and religious life. All divinely ordained states in life are beautiful and happy, when they are lived according to the gospel and lived generously. Jesus made this point strikingly in the concrete, semitic way of speaking. "A man's enemies will be those of his own household" (Mt 10:36 JB). Most human miseries arise from a lack of conversion. Evidence abounds. Every state in life entails sacrifice, of course—any noble life does. And at the same time every state in life, when it is lived according to the owner's manual, brings fulfillment and joy—in this case the owner's manual is of divine origin and it is interpreted rightly by the Church the Lord set up for this purpose. The problems in marriage or consecrated life or among the clergy are the people who are not living their vocations. It is then that the hellishness begins and grows. The solutions are the first six words of Jesus' public ministry: "Be converted and accept the Gospel."

Our second comment on the dismal expert views of wedded life is that marriage (and priesthood and religious life) are blessed vocations when the men and women concerned are deeply converted and enjoy profound intimacy with the Trinity. They are incomparably happier than those who are not. There is no bickering among them, no grudges, no scandals, no battles, physical or verbal. Major sins and minor pettinesses, cold silence and pouting disappear. When spouses disagree with each other, mutually receptive listening and amiable discussion replace impatient and snapping arguments. There is a genial pliability in nonessential matters, and when one slips, a generous forgiveness heals the momentary hurt. Am I describing an unreal utopia? No, indeed. Why am I so sure that the deeply converted are so happy? Three rock-like facts: (a) divine revelation: "rejoice in the Lord always"; (b) the lives of married, priestly and religious saints; (c) my own experience with contemporary persons in all three states of life—both those who are living them fully and faithfully, and those who are not. These are rock solid evidences. One does not argue intelligently with solid facts.

Hence, our first item of relevance and motivation for deep conversion is powerful: you will be far happier and fulfilled in your state in life, and so will those with whom you deal.

The Second Motive

This brings us to our second reason for perseveringly undertaking the arduous task of getting rid of our faults and sins. Here I shall be very direct, even a bit blunt. When I give retreats to married couples I address this issue head on: "You husbands and fathers say that you love your wives and children. OK, I am going to take you seriously. Now if you love them really (that is, for their genuine welfare and not simply for what you can get from them, or whether they do or do not return your love as you would like it to be returned)—I repeat, if you love them really, then prove it in the best way possible: become a saint, get rid of your faults, love totally. Why is this the best thing you can do for them? Your impact for their genuine, eternal welfare will be tremendous. Yes, you also show love for wife and children by putting bread on the table and a roof over their heads, but the best proof of genuine love is found in the example of an exemplary life: a tremendous spur to their eternal enthrallment, and yours as well."

Then I address the wives and mothers in the same direct manner: "You say you love your husband and children; then prove it in the best way possible: become a saintly wife, a saintly mother, etc." It is easy for spouses to use loving terms such as "darling, honey, sweetheart", but far more convincing is this down-to-earth proof in action.

Needless to say, but I shall say it, love in a priestly community and that of consecrated life is best proved not by endless meetings or in talking decade after decade about community. It is proved by giving a daily example of unselfish living, deep contemplative prayer, observing what one has vowed without the corrosive and divisive theological and liturgical disobediences or dissent which split communities and repel healthy young persons from joining them.

It is not foreign to our purpose to point out here that what we have been saying for the past page or two is exactly what spouses and religious who most need deep conversion are least willing to discuss. There is an elephant in the parlor, but they refuse to acknowledge its presence or to talk seriously about it. Let me illustrate with an example from religious life. When the members of a congregation speak of promoting vocations, they discuss endlessly new techniques to publicize their orders and plans for crafting catchy web sites. The real questions to ask are "Why are we not attracting our best young people? Could it be that our elegant dining and drinking and our secular clothes and hairdos and amusements repel them? Why are the orders who are obeying the Church's norms and teaching attracting so many?" These questions and others like them are the top priority issues. They are completely obvious to any honest person, but all the same there is a tacit agreement not to mention them. Similar types of unrealism happen in marriages in which deep conversion is lacking. The marriage or religious order in which the essential problems cannot be amiably discussed is to that extent dysfunctional. Full conversion is missing.

This then in our second item of relevance and motivation for profound conversion: by it we prove real love and offer to one another a daily example of eternal impact. We love with an effectiveness that promotes the other's eternal enthrallment as well as our own. This is real love, not in mere words, but in action.

The Third Reason for Deep Conversion

Our thought here has already been hinted at: since sin obscures sight, the more we are healed of our faults the better we see all else in the supernatural economy of salvation. It is a basic principle in the Scriptures that God gives his light to the humble and loving, two absolutely essential ingredients of conversion. Luke's account is especially charming. He notes that Jesus is filled with joy at the very thought of what he is going to share with the disciples. The Son was "filled with joy by the Holy Spirit", as he declared, "I bless you, Father, Lord of heaven and earth for hiding these things from the learned and clever and revealing them to mere children" (Lk 10:21 JB). Doctoral degrees are usually worthwhile, but they can trigger conceit in some people, and it is the conceit that is the problem. So also is vanity stemming from other gifts and accomplishments. It blocks insight into the most important of all human questions, the ultimate whys and hows of being fully beautiful and fulfilled. Love joins humility as the source of this superior light.

The beloved disciple makes this point in his first letter. As he admonishes the faithful to love one another he adds that "everyone who loves is begotten by God and knows God. Anyone who fails to love can never have known God, because God is love" (1 Jn 4:7–8 JB). Pastoral experience, and especially in spiritual direction, has made clear to me over and over again how people with a deepening prayer life (which happens as conversion deepens) understand far more readily the explanations one offers them.

The Fourth Reason

Our next item of relevance is ecumenical effectiveness. Because the gospel is without doubt the most beautiful worldview on our planet, when we live it fully, sincere people are mightily attracted to its beauty and to the Church. Jesus himself plainly said that it is by our love that the world will come to know that we are his disciples (Jn 13:35). A saint is a homilist without saying a word, a powerful proclamation of revealed truth and splendor. Throughout the centuries of our Catholic history it is the saints who attract the largest numbers to join us. Saint Francis of Assisi covered Europe with his friars. Saint Teresa of Avila was greeted by crowds when people heard that she and her nuns were on the way to their city to establish a new monastery. Saint John Vianney was like a huge magnet, drawing thousands to the privilege of confessing their sins to him. These men and women on fire needed no advertising to reach the multitudes. Pope John Paul II paraphrasing Saint Catherine of Siena (in her letter 368) remarked that "If you are what you should be, you will set the whole world ablaze." Saints do indeed light fires—and the reason is the title of this volume.

The Fifth Motive

As we move to our next bit of analysis, we may do well to pause and notice how all these reasons are so compelling that one of them alone would be more than sufficient to spark zealous efforts toward permanent change in a sincere person. Hence, we proceed on to number five. There is a mutual intercausality between deep conversion and deep prayer. They are not merely juxtaposed, one next to the other. Each one helps to bring about the other. The more we are rid of our egocentrisms the more we are opened to the divine infusions of love and intimacy. As Saint Paul puts it, we are transformed from one depth of beauty to another, a gift of the indwelling Spirit (2 Cor 3:18). In the other direction a progressively deepening of prayer furthers our purification from venial sins. Contemplative communion cannot be attained by any technique, oriental or occidental, nor by a centering method aimed at emptying the mind (see *Prayer Primer*, pp. 155–56). Saint Teresa was right on target when she commented that we cannot acquire "the least spark" of christic intimacy by techniques.

The Sixth Reason

A biblically inspired prayer from the Liturgy of the Hours nicely summarizes our sixth motive which should spark our desire for deep conversion: "All who seek you, Lord, will dance for joy" (Midmorning prayer, Wednesday, week 3). Though some may consider this biblically-based prayer an exaggeration, it is a result of a profound liberation from sin, even venial sin. Peter unhesitatingly proclaims to the faithful that "you are already filled with a joy so glorious that it cannot be described" (1 Pet 1:8). Yes, this happens on earth for those who have surrendered everything to love God totally, with no limit whatsoever—that is, for those who are deeply converted even to the transforming union itself. Hence, in a nutshell: why profound conversion? It triggers inexpressible joy. If one doubts this, let him try it.

Reason Number Seven

In our earliest catechism lessons we learned (or should have been taught) this final motive: namely, that in everything we do in this life we are making ourselves the kind of persons we shall be for all eternity: loving or hateful, egocentric or outgoing, fulfilled or frustrated, beautiful or ugly, ecstatically delighted or utterly miserable. Here on earth we begin to experience what will issue in eternal ecstasy or eternal disaster. And of course there are degrees of our eternal enthrallment. It would be nonsensical to give up even one degree of endless delight for a thousand paltry pleasures in this life, here one moment and gone the next. The Master put it perfectly: "What does it profit a man to gain the whole world and suffer the loss of his soul?" (Mt 16:26).

7

CONVERSION AND GENUINE LOVE

In our contemporary massive inundation of talk and chatter in the print and electronic media as well as in daily life, strong, beautiful words have, through overuse and sometimes abuse, often lost much of their accuracy and power. A prime example are two glories of the human race: freedom and choice. We alone in our vast cosmos write poetry and novels, history and philosophy, science and theology, because we alone have intellects and therefore freedom. We alone can be virtuous or guilty; plants and mere animals cannot. We invent and play chess, tennis, or football and build jumbo jets and computers—all because of these same powers of mind and soul. Palm trees and roses, squirrels and horses are not so fortunate. They are determined by nature and instinct.

Yet these two splendid words, freedom and choice, have now come to be used as euphemisms for the wanton destruction of innocent babies in their mothers' wombs. It is difficult to believe that advocates of abortion do not see that any sin is pro-choice, or it would not be a sin. The rapist is pro-choice, and so are the thief and adulterer and the liar. From a glorious word choice is now degraded to the level of a shameful cover-up. Examples of this abuse of language could be multiplied, of course, but we must turn to our main point.

Love is so splendid a word that the evangelist John used it to define the Lord of the universe himself: "God is love", unlimited, purest love (1 Jn 4:8). However, because dictionaries and thesauruses describe actual usage, it is not surprising that differing concepts of love abound in daily life. Among them we may note the following: a tender feeling of affection, a felt closeness due to kinship, feeling goodwill toward others, fondness and warmth, an attraction toward a gifted person, affection toward another along with a sexual attraction, passion and/or sexual intercourse, egocentric lust. A moment's reflection makes clear that with the exception of the last named, lust, all these usages either are or can be noble, depending on the circumstances and the motivation of the person concerned. For example, sexual relations in a committed marriage and according to the divine plan of welcoming children and forming them are indeed good.

Yet to see the full beauty of love we must turn to the gospel, for perfect love appeared on earth in all its splendor in the Incarnation of God's Son and in his life, words, Passion, death and Resurrection. Nowhere else do we find so incomparable a concept and reality. The gospel definition of love goes something like this: a self-sacrificing, willed concern for and giving to another, even if attraction and feeling are diminished or absent, and even if little or nothing is received in return—and all with divine motivation. To see fully the sublimity of this concept a few observations are necessary.

First of all, we notice that gospel love does not happen without conversion from egotism to a genuine love for truth, goodness and beauty. And deep love demands deep conversion. We give up our self-centeredness and seek the good of the ones we love. This altruism redounds to our own deeper welfare as well.

Secondly, the feeling element so common in the usual ideas about love may be diminished or absent even in the most authentic love. What is crucial is that our free will be operative. We do what ought to be done in given circumstances even when attraction, pleasure and inclination are absent. Genuine love is self-sacrificial.

Thirdly, we freely will and do all that should be done even when the other person does not reciprocate or return the favor or service—yes, even when no gesture or word of thanks is given. Indeed, we love even our enemies and return good for evil (Rom 12:14, 17, 21). The gospel is not simply an improvement on secular-minded ethics. It is a revolution.

Fourthly, this new love is immersed in a prior love for God from whom all lovableness in creation and in persons flows. This is why when we love our neighbor as we ought we are loving God himself. He is always endlessly lovable even when the neighbor is ugly, hurtful or an enemy. This is part and parcel with the fact that whatever is worthy of esteem in another person is due to his acceptance of divine gifts, while whatever is unloving is due to his free will rejecting those gifts.

The saints, glories of Catholicism, are heroic in their love just as they are heroic in all the virtues. Their lives are repeated pictures of what all this means concretely. Saint Francis Xavier kissing the leper and Saint Maximilian Kolbe substituting himself in the Nazi prison for the family man selected for execution are concrete models of what gospel self-giving looks like. So also is the mother caring for her infant baby who is in a terminal coma, even though she will receive no word of thanks in this life. Missionaries of Charity in Calcutta (and elsewhere) picking up dying men and women on the sweltering streets of a slum and showing them tender care in their dying hours are likewise presenting to all of us pictures of what we are attempting to explain in this chapter. So too are priests who imitate the saintly Curé of Ars and Padre Pio in their daily martyrdom of hours on end dispensing nonstop mercy in the confessional. Their profound love results from their profound conversion.

But the supreme example, the matchless exemplar of real love, is Jesus being slowly tortured to death on his Cross out of nothing but a total self-gift for you and me. The Crucifixion and all that went before it is, in our universe, the supreme horror and the supreme beauty. This is why a crucifix is so precious in Catholicism. "Greater love than this no man has but to lay down his life for his friends" (Jn 15:13). Hans Urs von Balthasar put it well when he somewhere wrote that "it is face to face with Christ crucified that the abysmal egoism of what we are accustomed to call love becomes clear". This is a strong statement, but not an exaggeration. The usual idea of love is often self-centered. "He/she/it attracts me. I find pleasure in him/her/it. Therefore I love." All one has to do to see the point is to compare the world's usages of the term (as we find them in a large dictionary or a thorough thesaurus) with a simple crucifix. One's reaction before the latter should be speechless gazing, pondering, adoring. No one in history or in fiction begins to compare with the Lord of glory on his Cross: the splendor of his person, his message, his love.

Love Rooted in Conversion: Conclusions

Several consequences follow from this christic love. The first is that it takes a radical conversion in us to come to be able to love another genuinely, even a beautiful person.

Being attracted to stunning beauty can be good, but it is not automatically love. Even a wretched pervert can be attracted. If that beauty should lessen or be lost entirely, would there still be a selfless response to the person's need? In other words, attraction toward others does not become love until we have accepted the christic message and also been cleansed of self-seeking—then genuine love is possible.

Our second conclusion follows closely from the first: because it takes conversion to be able to love another, it takes deep conversion to love that person deeply. If husbands and wives understood this and put it into practice, divorces would vanish. And so would domestic fights and bickering and pouting and shouting disappear. Sympathetic listening to each other in differences of opinion would blossom. Each spouse would desire to do what the other prefers in practical matters. When one slips through half-advertence or momentary weakness, loving forgiveness would bring immediate healing. The children would see and experience what genuine family life looks like. Even though it may be a gradual and even slow process, they, too, would begin to practice what they see. Yes, christic love is a revolution. This second conclusion (as well as all of them) applies as well to convents, monasteries, rectories, nursing homes—wherever people live closely.

Our third consequence may be briefly expressed: there is no such thing as love at first sight. Yes, there are on occasion strong attractions at first sight, noble or ignoble. But from all we have said it is obvious that, while the worldly world may consider an attraction to be love, far, far more is required for the genuine article.

Conclusion number four is surprising only to those who have given little serious attention to the demands of genuine love or have not profited from their experience of the real world. Some years ago I came across a psychologist (whose name I do not recall) who wrote that a capacity for genuine love between the sexes is rare. I ask the reader to notice that he did not say merely that love between the sexes is rare—a capacity, the basic ability to love is rare. Even though he was not writing from a religious point of view, he was surely on to something. He may not have known why it is rare, but the New Testament explains that nicely. In his first letter Saint Peter notes that two conditions must be fulfilled before real love happens. We must accept divine revelation and then be purified of our defects. "You have been obedient to the truth and purified your souls until you can love like brothers, in sincerity; let your love for each other be real and from your heart" (1 Pet 1:22 JB). Real love is uncommon in our world because full conversion is uncommon.

Finally, it follows from all the above that heroic conversion begets heroic love. The saints are perfect illustrations. For those who may have some lingering doubts, I would suggest simply that they read historically-sound lives of these remarkable men and women.

Deep Love Is Coterminous with Deep Prayer

Heroic love for God and neighbor is, of course, closely allied to profound intimacy with the indwelling Trinity. To a large extent they are the same thing. We love Father, Son and Holy Spirit to the extent that we are in an intimate prayer communion with them which is lived out in our actions. And we have a vibrant love for our neighbors (spouse, children, friends, co-workers, parishioners) to the extent that we love God. The first and second commandments cannot be separated—as both Scripture and life experiences make clear.

The best way to see how contemplative intimacy and love

are the same reality is to look at the radiant image of the Father, Jesus himself (Heb 1:3). He habitually spent hours "long before dawn" deeply absorbed in the Father, and even on occasion it was the whole night in this profound communion (Mk 1:35; Lk 5:16; 6:12). He obviously was totally in love with his Father, for the Father was always present to him (Jn 16:32). Indeed his deepest love was coterminous with his deepest prayer.

Both testaments of Scripture take it for granted that deep love and deep prayer are to be found in everyone's life. The one thing we ask, the one thing we seek is to gaze on the beauty of the Lord (Ps 27:4); that is, the most important of all human activities is to be immersed in contemplative intimacy with God. What else could this be but a divinely profound love? We are to taste and see for ourselves, to experience a deep delight in this interpersonal closeness, a union that makes us radiant with joy (Ps 34:5, 8). So absorbing does this communion become that one's awareness, the eyes of one's mind, are always on the Lord (Ps 25:15). Not surprisingly, this love communion sparks an amazing thirsting for the living God as a deer longs for the flowing waters. One sings to the Beloved through the night, pining for him as a parched desert thirsts for the refreshing rain (Ps 42:1-2; 63:1). This intimacy brings with it a joy so great that it cannot be described (1 Pet 1:8), and it transforms the person from one glory to another (2 Cor 3:18). It can grow to a point where it fills a person "with the utter fullness of God" (Eph 3:19 JB), a staggering statement when one reflects on it for a few minutes.

The fact that the Church in her liturgy repeatedly places these texts and others like them on the lips of all the faithful is a clear indication that deep conversion, love and communion with God are bound together in a unity meant for all states in life. Then, too, Vatican Council II expressly taught that we are all called to contemplative prayer and a burning love for the Trinity (SC, nos. 2 and 10). The Lord's statement to Blessed Angela of Foligno applies likewise to all of us: "Make yourself a capacity and I will make myself a torrent." With his grace we open ourselves by deep conversion and he eagerly pours out by his Spirit a deluge of love (Rom 5:5).

Saints Light Fires

Painstaking and thoroughgoing student of ecclesiastical history that he was, John Henry Newman astutely observed that large groups of people, even large groups of religiously-minded people, do not light fires. Throughout the Church's twenty centuries of history, it is individuals who ignite the blazes. Examples abound both through the centuries and in our own contemporary experience. Government bodies, town hall meetings, boards of directors on occasion promote worthy projects and programs. General chapters and other meetings of religious orders (assemblies of a province, local and regional meetings) likewise can both hinder and further genuine progress, but these groups seldom, if ever, do anything that looks like a conflagration. If the group is blessed to have a saint in its midst, something great may happen—unless the group manages to thwart even a saint with majority mediocrity. It is men and women like Augustine, Chrysostom, Benedict, Bernard, Francis, Dominic, Catherine, Thomas, Ignatius, Teresa of Avila, John of the Cross, John Vianney and Thérèse of Lisieux who light the fires. The evidence is convincing.

The glories of Church history are chiefly the works of individuals who, themselves bursting with love and intimacy with the Trinity, spark others to imitate their burning love, their magnanimity and their heroicity in all the virtues. At the same time it is their deep love intimacy with the Lord that is the taproot of their ability to heal human hurts. These, too, have been with us through the centuries—nor are they lacking in our secularized world living under the burden and threats of fanatical terrorism.

8

CONFLICTS AND CONVERSION

Even aside from physical pains and illnesses, all of us ordinary folk are hurting in various ways and in differing degrees. The hurts derive from our own mistakes and sins, as well as from others' errors, indifference, unkindnesses, even betrayals and verbal abuse (if not physical). Some of us are wounded deeply with lasting scars, others in lesser ways. We should, of course, offer and accept healing compassion to and from others. Yet from all available evidence, the most basic healing of our deepest wounds comes from contemplative intimacy with the indwelling Trinity and the deep conversion that makes it possible. This last sentence is far from obvious to everyone. It is the aim of this chapter to explain how and why it is true. Some analysis is in order.

First of all, we should understand that human hurts are not caused by states in life. Marriage is not faulty; husbands and wives are the problems. The same is true of clergy and consecrated life. People who are not living a life as it is meant to be lived should expect the painful consequences of their aberrations. Each state in life is of divine origin and is good, beautiful and healing. It works well if it is lived well. The most painful suffering is not caused by vocations. The main problems are with people in the vocation who are not living it according to the divine plan for that way of life. Jesus made this point explicitly when he pointed out that the chief enemies of a household are right in the home itself (Mt 10:36).

Secondly, sound psychology and competent counseling can be helpful in healing human hurts, but they are greatly limited—as anyone with much experience in the field well knows. Severely wounded people often need professional therapy. Yet all the same, these psychological resources frequently do not get to root causes.

A recent cover story in *Time* magazine illustrated this very point. Raising the question whether a good marriage can be taught, the article contrasted the results of the therapy model and the education model. "Every system sounds great—until you ask other marriage specialists about it . . . [W]hen experts start comparing claims and stats, you hear the cacophony of rival used-car salesmen. Is it the therapists who need education? Or is it the Marriage Education folks who need therapy?" The conclusion is not encouraging: "At a time when America's married and soon-to-bes are eager for mediation, the bickering of the two sides is unhelpful" (January 19, 2004, n.p.).

The Main Roots of Human Conflicts

That we may avoid oversimplifications we immediately acknowledge that there are minor sources of human arguments and disturbances. Among these obviously are errors, mistakes and misunderstandings from innocent statements and actions. What we have in mind at the moment are the chief roots of our hurts, disagreements and sufferings deriving from our interactions and in our relationships with one another.

Each of us from the date of our birth experiences an egocentric outlook and behavior whose origin stems from our aboriginal woundedness. There is no other adequate explanation. We are born into this world utterly self-centered, and it is only after long struggling that some of us manage to get rid of it, partially or wholly. In theology we call this fundamental wound original sin. As Chesterton rightly noted, its reality is as clear as it could be. Anyone who knows himself at all knows it to be true.

This egoism shows itself in myriads of suppositions, minor and major: "I won't be patient with your ways of doing things and your faults, but I expect you to be patient with mine . . . You must accommodate my desires and preferences, but I need not accommodate yours . . . You should understand my idiosyncrasies, but I need not understand yours . . . When we disagree, I need not be gentle and amiable and open-minded, but you must be all of these." With this egotistic attitude on the part of one or both parties there will be, of course, frequent conflicts with endless arguing and bickering. Psychology does not, and cannot, cure this root of conflict. The only remedy is conversion, deep conversion. And this happens only with God's grace and our surefire program—or it does not happen. Saints are unanswerable evidence.

The second main root of conflict is seldom even noticed in our day. It is called illuminism. As far as I can tell, the idea is practically unknown in secular circles, and yet the reality is not rare. The word, illuminism, comes from the Latin for light: *lumen*. This illness, and it is part of the original wound, comes in two forms. On the natural level it is the conviction of some people that their ideas, their opinions, their preferences are automatically superior to those of others. When one talks to an illuminist, evidence contrary to the latter's view has little or no effect on his conviction.

Even if the evidence is objectively compelling, it does not penetrate his mind or will. This is natural illuminism.

On the supernatural level this disease shows itself in the conviction that "I have a special light from the Holy Spirit; you do not. Therefore, I am right and you are wrong." I like to call this form of the aberration the privileged-pipeline-to-God idea. One can present to this person objective evidence from reason, Scripture, the teaching Church, brilliant theologians, and, once again, no dent is made on the illuminist's mind. The reaction is the same: "I know better; you are wrong." If the reader wishes a 600-page historical study of illuminism, he can find it in Ronald Knox's *Enthusiasm*. It is clear that disagreements with an illuminist spouse, relative, friend, fellow worker or parishioner will go nowhere until humility enters the picture—and that requires conversion. Psychology may help somewhat, but it cannot bring about the inner transformation we are talking about in this volume.

The third main root of hurts and conflicts is a lack of perspective, a lack of proportion in viewing and acting upon problems that commonly arise when people gather together. For those of us who are not saintly, it is very difficult to see big things as big and small things as small—especially when there is question of our preferences. Many people never do make significant progress, especially in matters that annoy them. Spouses can easily get into a bitter and mean argument about almost nothing (a lack of tidiness, coming late, a minor complaint, spending an extra hour with the computer or at the bridge club). Of course these faults should be corrected, but that is not the issue at the moment. The point is that the fault is minor compared to what is major: namely, that they genuinely love each other even in their disagreement and that they are gentle and loving in their discussion of it.

The final root of suffering in communal life is a lack of what the New Testament calls having "one mind", or as we now term it, a shared vision about the main issues of life: God, religion, why we exist at all, the principles of morality, the nature of one's state in life and its obligations, a balanced use of money, chastity, raising of children, what real love is and is not. If spouses or members of consecrated institutes are at odds about these fundamentals, it is no surprise that they are in continual conflict, spoken or unspoken. We have here another reason why marriage counselors will say things like, "All couples fight" or "The average husband and wife have a battle on average about once a month." Saints do not fight at all (in this sense). Once again the New Testament therapy alone works adequately. The conflicts of which we are speaking in this chapter are fully healed or cease only when deepening conversion happens.

The only people I notice in our societies who pursue the ideal of shared vision are those who take the christic gospel seriously. Democratic governments do not even consider the ideal possible. Totalitarian regimes stifle and crush any group that disagrees with them. The atheists I have read do not speak of it at all, nor does what I have read of Buddhism, Hinduism and Islam. Islam, throughout most of its history, has tried to impose one mind by force, persecution, blood-shed and execution, but that "unity" is pseudo, and light-years from shared vision, which by its very nature cannot be forced.

This gospel picture of beautiful human community is not only largely absent from secular thinking, it is not nearly as prominent in our popular Christian milieu as it ought to be. We will therefore offer here a few brief thoughts on the subject. They present a picture of deep conversion in practice and a sketch of something our society drastically needs. If one wishes a book-length treatment of this theme, he may consult the author's *Caring: A Biblical Theology of Community*.

Presuppositions to Attaining Shared Vision

As we have just indicated above, the gospel ideal of "one mind" cannot be forced. Nor does it arise out of the blue because good people want to be "united in mind and heart" (Acts 4:32). Yes, sensible people want this. But mere wishes and velleities are not the same thing as profound conversion. Beginning with Jesus' brilliant six-word introduction to his public ministry (recorded in Mk 1:15; see Chapter 2, above), this book has prepared us to benefit from a brief summary of what we term above the New Testament therapy for the divisions and conflicts so rampant in contemporary primary communities and in our world at large.

Since wishes and velleities cannot produce one mind and one heart, we ask how does this beautiful ideal come about in actual life? How can free people be in touch with reality (the classical concept of truth) together? How can they be united in their basic grasp of things as they are? What are the presuppositions of shared vision?

The first need is that we have a genuine love for one another (for a reminder of what genuine love means see our previous Chapter 7). Those who have a real love yearn to be of one mind with the beloved. If I do not care what you think about the most important realities, I should admit that my love is close to zero. As Saint Paul put it, "Do everything you can to preserve unity"—which in his mind includes a unity of intellect as well as will (Eph 4:3; 1 Cor 1:10). Governments that persecute their citizens and a religion that tries to grow by the sword obviously are not prompted by love. Forced conversions are illusory.

The second condition for shared vision to happen is a real love for truth, that is, for things as they actually are. Love for one's preferences and desires without care for objective evidence is egocentric and will never bring oneness of mind about basic things. We have already dealt with the sole cure for this type of selfishness.

Thirdly, attaining an interpersonal unity of mind requires that both parties welcome correction (which of course should be both honest and gentle). The scriptural program offers what psychology would usually not dare to say: "Teach and admonish one another in all wisdom" (Col 3:16) . . . "Correct an arrogant man, you get insult in return. Correct a wise man and he will love you for it . . . He grows wiser still" (Prov 9:7–9). All of which makes huge sense. If I love truth I will appreciate learning from another of my faults and errors, and I will love the one who points them out. No one will doubt for a moment that this rare humility requires no little conversion. Psychology alone and secular mores will not do the trick. Once again revelation is right.

Our next presupposition we have just mentioned, but it needs a bit more attention. I refer to humility. The vain person is not in the least inclined to be corrected by another. He assumes that his knowledge and judgment are superior, and he sees himself to have few or no faults worth mentioning. Hence, this individual is constantly at odds with husband or wife or others in shop or office. Yet Jesus makes it plain that we do not have his wisdom unless we are innerly transformed. He gives his light to the humble and resists the proud (Lk 10:21). The book of Proverbs made it clear centuries earlier that the individual who trusts his own promptings, his own desires, is a fool (Prov 28:26). Humble men and women are ready to receive the light of the Holy Spirit, and consistently enough, they have one mind, given to them by the source of all that is true and good and beautiful, the triune God (Jas 1:17).

The fifth condition for a close unity of mind and heart in any community is giving up our own mere likes and preferences, which often are what Saint Paul calls "illusory desires" (Eph 4:22–23). Many if not most daily arguments and bickerings at home, in the marketplace, wherever people live together are due to this clinging: "it must be my way and my preferences, what I like and what I want." Mere gimmicks cannot free us from these wounds.

Our last presupposition is that the members of a community together drink from the same fountains of unity. Saint Thomas Aquinas pointed out what should be obvious to any thoughtful person on a few moments of reflection: unity is always caused. It never happens by random chance. Our universe is full of evidence that this is true. The unity of a Pietà or a Mozart symphony cannot arise from the swirling of trillions of molecules of marble or musical notations flying about at random for millions of years. The suggestion is ludicrous and everyone knows it. A jumbo jet with its millions of parts, including computer parts, could not arise from a cosmic storm of diverse atoms and molecules which finally resulted in this massively intricate flying masterpiece with no intellects behind it. Once again everyone knows this intuitively and compellingly.

It is amusing how scientists, when they find a written text

amid ancient ruins, are immediately certain that the author of these ideas or laws was no mere animal, but rather an intellectual being, a man or a woman. Yet it must be either philosophical incompetence or extraordinary stubbornness that would lead them to deny that an endlessly more complex reality like a living cell comes from an intellectual being. The reason cannot be science. It is a philosophical monism, a dogmatic materialism. And of course materialism is pure philosophy, not science. The dogma here, with no foundation in reality, is that materialists are forbidden by their philosophy to accept the compelling conclusion of a supreme intellect behind an awesomely complex and stunning universe.

So also in human communities, if the members accept clear and objective evidence and thus drink from the same fountains of unity, they will have one mind. In this case the fountains are God's revelation and the guidance of the Church he authorized to teach eternal and moral matters in his name. When husbands and wives, when members of any primary community learn from the same sources of truth, understandably they possess the same basic truths. No one is forced. But once again, the beautiful unity happens only as a result of sincere inner change.

New Testament Rootings

We should perhaps now give a brief sketch of what we have been assuming in this chapter, namely that this happy wisdom, largely unknown in other worldviews, comes from divine revelation. The Gospels and apostolic writings clearly require shared vision among the members of Jesus' Church and in all states of life. A rapid outline will suffice.

At the last supper Jesus prayed that his disciples would be "completely one", a trait so unusual in fact that their unity would be a miracle to the world (Jn 17:23). Indeed what we have been describing is so rare that we find it in no other worldview. The saints live it, and they are themselves miracles. They in the greatest freedom have heroic virtue and consequently the perfect unity of mind, convictions and aims to which Saint Paul exhorts the Corinthians and the Philippians (1 Cor 1:10; Phil 2:1–2).

Fully honest, as was his wont, Paul also makes it clear that a divided community—in marriage, parish, religious community—is worldly and immature. Divisions are caused by sin (1 Cor 3:1–3; Gal 5:19–21). Startling as that may be to people who consider arguing, bickering and fighting to be normal, serious thought makes it clear, especially in the light of what we have already considered in this study.

Perhaps more startling still is Jesus' pronouncement that a community which is divided is doomed to failure. A town or household split into factions cannot last for long (see Mt 12:25). Contemporary evidence abounds that shows he is right again. The very word divorce means breaking or splitting up, sundering apart. Polarized religious institutes have been declining at an alarming rate for some decades now, and not a few are either on the brink of disappearing altogether or have already vanished. Jewish scholar Will Herberg has remarked that "no movement in the Catholic Church in twenty centuries has had lasting success without or against papal support." History coincides with sound theology—they tell the same sad story.

Without doubt the most successful plan for preventing and for permanently healing human conflicts and hurts is expressed in the title of this volume. This is a strong statement to be sure, and the credit for it goes not to the author but to the divine revelation on which it is entirely based. One may not argue intelligently with this claim without examining the evidence for it, and very few outside the Church seem to have looked at the best of experimental evidence, the saints and those who imitate them closely. These heroes of human goodness simply do not inflict wounds on others—and very often, indeed day in and day out, they heal the deepest of human sufferings. One thinks immediately of Blessed Teresa of Calcutta and her Sisters. These women and other consecrated religious like them, are simply carrying out fully the gospel program of what christic holiness and healing look like.

We need to look a bit more closely at this therapy. Once again we can offer here only a sketch. A fuller picture can be found in the same book we have already referred to above. So we ask: What is the gospel message about interpersonal relationships in marriage, religious life, priesthood, yes, even in shops and offices, hospitals and nursing homes? It is a revolution, a divinely instigated revolution (Eph 4:23).

Caring Concern

We may begin with two examples of this revolution. When Saint Paul addresses the members of the early Church in Rome, he calls them "God's beloved" (Rom 1:7). Since we are to love one another as the Lord loves us (Jn 13:34–35), we conclude that other people are to be our beloved—in the most genuine sense of the word! How often does that happen in homes, shops, offices, or in the supermarket checkout line? To the Philippians the Apostle writes that "nobody [is to] think of his own interests first but everybody is to think of other people's interests instead" (Phil 2:4 JB). What we do find in our world is indifference, criticism, hostility, even in some countries outright hatred toward outsiders, along with persecution and bloodshed. In these places the christic revolution has not even begun.

Shown Warmth

When children are brought to Jesus for a blessing, he hugs each one (Mk 10:16). When a young man comes for advice and then refuses it, even though the Lord had "looked at him with love" (Mk 10:21), we are seeing warm love in action. When the prodigal son returns from using half of his father's fortune with prostitutes, the father "ran to the boy, clasped him in his arms and kissed him tenderly" (Lk 15:20 JB); we have still another astonishing example. This one sentence along with the whole parable is not only a literary masterpiece; it has the divine handwriting all over it. After Pentecost the apostles imitate their Master in showing this astonishingly warm affection. Saint Paul tells his Philippians how he prays for them with joy, how they have a permanent place in his heart, how he misses every one of them, "loving you as Christ Jesus loves you" (Phil 1:3-8). Peter closes his first letter in advising its recipients to "greet one another with the kiss of love" (1 Pet 5:14; see also 2 Cor 2:4-8 and Phil 4:1). It takes no vivid imagination to see why in these pages I have made the comment more than once: there is no other worldview that comes close to the beauty of the Lord and his teaching . . . and our saints who live it to the utmost. In noting this we are not praising ourselves, but the Master and the Church he founded which keeps and proclaims that message without dilution.

Overcoming Evil with Good

With the exception of Jesus and his Mother, all of us have been wounded by the original fall, as well as by our own sins and those of others against us. We all need healing in differing ways and to differing degrees. If we are faithful to our christic heritage, we do not react to evil with more evil. Saint Paul three times in one chapter in his letter to the Romans beautifully points out that we respond to persecution by blessing our persecutors, we react to something wrong with something good, we overcome evil with good (Rom 12:14, 17, 21). This is exactly how Jesus himself responded to the most horrendous and monstrous evil the universe has ever seen: God himself being tortured to death in his Passion and on the Cross. We have already noted how this ghastly wickedness is also the supreme beauty of perfect love.

But how do we lesser ones live this lofty message in the concrete specifics of our daily lives? We begin the process of overcoming evil with good by forgiveness, unlimited forgiveness (Mt 18:21–22). The other person is to stop offending, of course: "Go and sin no more." We recall that this forgiveness is an act of the will which we can control with grace. It is compatible with continuing to feel hurt and/or the feeling of resentment which we usually cannot control.

Next we pray for the perpetrators of the wrong; for their genuine good and welfare, and that they repent and change their behavior. Third, we give them an example in our own behavior of what the gospel looks like: no retaliation, no grudge-keeping, no animosity, no shown bitterness, no refusal to communicate and talk.

Fourth, when something is wrong with another person, we do not gossip about the fault or (usually) go to the person in charge as the first step, but to the person himself, "and keep it between your two selves" (Mt 18:15 JB). If the offender is also trying to live the gospel, he welcomes the admonition (which should be offered gently and be motivated by love). Hopefully he does not explode with indignation (Prov 9:7–9). Each one genuinely listens sympathetically to the other's view of the matter. They both change for the better. People who are deeply converted live this way. They overcome evil with good. If everyone were to accept and practice this divine revelation, the wounds of our world would be vastly lessened. What could be more obvious?

Summary in a Nutshell

This magnificent picture of human communities—marriages, consecrated life, parishes and all others—comes about when profound inner changes and a deep intimacy with God come about. Human ideas and psychological counseling may offer some help, but on the whole, without the gospel therapy, the healing is partial at best: "Love one another as I have loved you." Not something less.

9

A SUREFIRE PROGRAM

When a serious person reflects on what we have considered in Chapter 5 about our remarkable resistance to deep conversion, it is not surprising that a kind of feeling of hopelessness may set in. How does it happen that people who have given up deadly sins and basically do love God at least in some minimal way can yet continue to cling to petty selfishnesses even if only in three or four areas? Why do they cling especially in matters that concern interpersonal relations and the pleasures of a comfortable lifestyle? Despite a regular reception of the sacrament of reconciliation and perhaps a fidelity to annual retreats, they change little from one decade to another. I should like to think that this type of person usually does not positively decide "I do not intend to improve . . . I want my mediocrity . . . I don't want to get better." Hopefully these protestations are rare among religiously-minded people. But the fact remains that frequently in these people willed and habitual venial sins continue on in their lives: gossiping, laziness, overeating, snapping at one another—to mention just a few examples. There is no determined, persevering effort to throw them overboard, and of course, no lasting decision to practice heroic virtue, to live as the saints live.

Most of us will grant that this is true. What is also true is that by ourselves we can do nothing salutary, let alone be converted. Saint Paul made that plain: "No one can say, 'Jesus is Lord' unless he is under the influence of the Holy Spirit" (1 Cor 12:3 JB). But we are not alone. With divine aid, always offered but never forced, we can and should aspire to saintliness. This aspiration is called the virtue of magnanimity: aiming at doing great things for God and for those he loves so much—which means for everyone.

"Well, then," you may ask, "how does deep conversion happen? My track record is poor, extremely poor. God wants to give, but as you just noted, he never forces us against our will. What is going to get me to move? And to be persevering about it? Not just for a few weeks after I finish this book, but for the whole rest of my life?" Fine questions.

This chapter provides answers. We here offer a surefire program. No gimmicks, psychological or otherwise. Clever tricks and catchy phrases do not and cannot bring about profound personal and persevering changes for the better. Remember: our resistance is remarkable.

So what is our part in seeing to it that deep conversion does come about in our individual lives? This we shall explain with a series of Be's: Be concerned. Be determined. Be committed to meditative and contemplative prayer. Be motivated. Be humble. Be specific. Be persevering. A suggestion: You might put this book down right now and ponder these seven Be's and wonder to yourself how they apply to you. See what you can make of them before you read on. It may take you ten minutes or an hour, but it will be time well spent. Your pondering may ready you to get more from what we now have to say.

Later: If you are one of those rare persons who have little to worry about, our first Be is tailor made for you. And if you do have other worries, it is still made for you. It is made for all of us ordinary people.

Be Concerned

One of the typical traits of morally mediocre people is their feeling a cozy at-home-ness with their illness. Why is moral lukewarmness a malady? (See the scathing rebukes in Rev 3:1–18.) Healthy things grow. They develop to maturity, to full perfection according to their kind. A rose bud that does not open has something wrong with it. So also an acorn that sprouts no stems, no leaves, will never become a mighty oak. A senior in high school who reads at the sixth-grade level is retarded at least as regards accomplishment, if not in talent.

Baptized men and women are living a life, a new life, the supreme life that gives meaning, a glorious meaning that is the reason for our huge universe. God pays us the compliment of calling us to live that life fully, perfectly, to be transformed from one glory to another (Mt 5:48; 2 Cor 3:18). We are meant to be filled with the utter fullness of endless Beauty, and finally to be unspeakably enthralled in the beatific vision in risen body (Eph 3:19; 1 Cor 2:9).

Willingly to be lagging on the way, knowingly to snuff out sparks of grace is an enormous reason for concern. If one wishes something to be bothered about, the number one candidate is the freely chosen and eternal disaster of losing the eternal enthrallment and falling into that state whose usual name is hell. The number two possibility is moral mediocrity, the willed refusal to become the beautiful person to which each of us is invited.

Saints make neither of these tragic blunders. They burningly pursue deep conversion and deep love. For them anything less is not enough. Saint John Vianney, the famous Curé of Ars, was a martyr to the confessional. He sat in that tiny box for ten to eighteen hours each day for decade after decade and with no vacation. The church was neither air-conditioned in the summer nor heated in the winter, and there he was confined, hearing over and over and over again the woes of mankind: listening, explaining, advising, persuading, healing endless streams of sinners. Facing a firing squad once would be far easier. Yet this same priest, immeasurably more self-giving, more loving, more penitential than the least of us, was not satisfied with his degree of conversion and love. When he was about seventy years old, he wanted to leave his parish and go to a solitude so that he could "weep for my life". This priest was a perfect, a heroic picture of what "to be concerned" actually means. He was light-years beyond the mediocre worldling.

A second illustration of "Be concerned" appeared in the press a few years ago. Pope John Paul II, during one of his international trips, had taken to bed with a fever. Perhaps too soon (for some people) he wanted to resume his taxing schedule. One of the Polish Sisters who cared for domestic matters at the Vatican expressed her concern at his decision: "I am worried about your Holiness," she remarked. He immediately responded, "I too am worried about my holiness." Most people rightly admired John Paul II for his fearless proclamation of the truth and his wholehearted living of it. Yet he was concerned that there was yet more he should be giving. He was concerned about his living the gospel more fully yet.

If you and I aspire to be deeply converted and to love generously, we had better be bothered about the level we have thus far reached or not reached. And we ought not to forget the divine rebuke: since you are "only lukewarm, I will spit you out of my mouth" (Rev 3:16 JB).

Be Determined

It is safe to say that when we hear of world-class performances in scholarship, music, art, science or sports, many of us assume that these accomplishments are due mainly to rare natural talents and gifts. While there may be a lonely exception, studies of this question say otherwise. An article syndicated by the *Los Angeles Times* in 1985 reported that "A five-year study of 120 of the nation's top artists, athletes and scholars has concluded that drive and determination, not great natural talent, led to their extraordinary success." The article then went on to give striking examples of this determination from their background research into the careers in six fields: "concert pianists, Olympic swimmers, sculptors, tennis players, mathematicians and research neurologists". Thomas Edison had put these findings in one short sentence: "Genius is 1 percent inspiration and 99 percent perspiration."

Studies of the saints yield the same conclusion regarding their sanctity. A few of them were highly talented, even geniuses: Augustine, Aquinas, Bellarmine. Others like the Curé of Ars were ordinary in natural gifts, even on occasion, limited. We may go further and notice that on the natural level the saints on their own begin their lives as weak as the rest of us. The preface of the Mass of martyrs puts the matter perfectly. Addressing God, the Church proclaims "You choose the weak of this world and make them strong."

A natural lethargy plus our original woundedness and persistent selfish clingings shown in repeated venial sins provide an abundance of experiential evidence that, without determination and solid repentance, the second and third degrees of conversion simply will not happen. God's grace is needed, of course—we are not Pelagians. But he does not force anyone's will. He makes the weak of this world mighty only to the extent that they cooperate with a determined and resolute repentance. Given that the first and second degrees of conversion do not occur without a firm will, all the more is this true of heroic virtue. People who know their own weaknesses know this only too well.

Be Motivated

All of our Be's are interlinked and interwoven, as a moment's reflection makes clear. Being vibrantly concerned is the first step toward a strong determination to do something about the problem. And to be driven with persevering determination requires motivation, clear and compelling incentives.

In Chapter 6, "Relevance and Motivation", we considered seven reasons why deep conversion and deep prayer are absolutely essential to becoming a completely loving, happy and fulfilled human person. A periodic review of these reasons, almost committing them to rote memory, would provide a continuing thrust on the hard but happy road. If they fade away in our mind, determination will weaken and probably disappear.

At this point we offer four more reasons to bolster volitional impact. Our eighth motive therefore is the realization that our apostolic effectiveness will be immensely increased in proportion as we grow from the first degree of conversion, through the second and on to the third crowning transformation. By apostolates here we include not only proclaiming the gospel, administering the sacraments and nursing the sick in priesthood and consecrated life, but we envision also lay men and women witnessing to truth, love and beauty by the example of their lives in shops and offices, in board rooms and government agencies, in schools and universities, in doctors' offices and nursing homes, on athletic fields and courts. We decidedly include also spouses in their homes witnessing to each other and to their children and their extended families and friends.

To bring people closer to God, competency and clarity are important, but they are not enough. Of themselves they do not touch hearts deeply. Personal sanctity and goodness do. It is the saints who light fires. There is a direct correlation between the beauty of holiness and the fruitfulness of our work and interpersonal relationships. Lay theologian and eloquent speaker Frank Sheed knew this not only theoretically but also from personal experience. He proclaimed the gospel and the Church's teaching of it in the most difficult of circumstances, that is, perched on a soap box in the midst of bystanders in London's Hyde Park. Here is how he put this motive in his book, *The Church and I*, p. 65:

> Teaching science or mathematics, even history or literature, the main thing is to be lucid. But for ideas which could call upon a man to change his life, lucidity is not enough. The self of the teacher has to make contact in depth with the self of the hearer. To say that the speaker must give himself with the truth adhering may sound pretentious, espccially if you have in mind the standard picture of the soap box orator. But it is the minimum. The speaker and his message reach the hearer together. If the hearer finds the speaker repellent, the message hasn't a hope—it arrives discolored by, smelling of the one who uttered it.

There are a few people objective and honest enough to accept solid evidence for some moral or religious idea aside from who is speaking (Augustine, Newman and Chesterton come to mind), but unfortunately in matters of one's way of life most go by their preferences, not by objective reasons.

This is sad but true. If we are going to bring people closer to God in work and life our own deepening conversion is indispensable.

As we have already noted, if husbands and wives really love each other and their children, the best and most effective proof that their love is not mere words is to get rid of their major and minor selfishnesses and to deepen their prayer lives. Then the salutary effects of what is done snowball. It goes without saying that this is true also for bishops, priests and members of consecrated life. There is no substitute for authenticity.

The ninth motive for embracing our entire surefire program may surprise you: people who are profoundly intimate with their indwelling Lord are never bored. This I have learned both from experience in daily life and in the spiritual direction of those who are close to God. In the first century Saint Peter was able to say to his newly baptized Catholics (who apparently had already made considerable progress in holiness), "You did not see him, yet you love him, and still without seeing him, you are filled with a joy so glorious that it cannot be described" (1 Pet 1:8 JB). Boredom and genuine joy are incompatible. Selfishness diminishes a person's liveliness and capacity to enjoy reality and to grow in the best of human relationships. Egotism is a self-centered dead-end.

Our tenth reason for taking the path to lofty virtue is that it equips the person to handle suffering profitably and even happily. Saint Paul hit the nail on the head: "For those who love God everything works together for good" (Rom 8:28). Yes, even illness, criticism or failure bring blessings to one who embraces these negatives of life in union with Jesus tortured to death on the Cross. The saints experience this continuously in their lives, whereas those who choose to get bitter and cynical in their hardships become more and more miserable.

Our final motivation for resolute determination is that by it we are building up our primary community: marriage, priesthood, consecrated life. A moment's reflection makes this obvious. We recall once again that Jesus made this point clear: Our chief enemies are members of our own household (Mt 10:36). Outsiders can do us harm, but far greater damage is usually brought about by spouses who refuse to get rid of their sins. The same is true in the rectory or convent, of parishes and nursing homes. Life is far more harmonious and happy among people who readily renounce their egocentrisms. By giving up everything, they gain everything.

Be Committed to Daily Meditative/Contemplative Prayer

We come now to the taproot of our surefire program: intimacy with the indwelling Trinity. To put it simply: the main source of deep conversion is to fall in love with endless Beauty. A genuine person will gladly sacrifice for real love. Christic martyrs are in love. Jesus tortured to death on the Cross is the icon of perfect love, unconditional, selfless love. All the saints imitate him in their heroic virtue because they too are in love. Their concern, determination, and motivation are rooted in and arise from their intimacy with triune Beauty who is purest and endless love (cf. 1 Jn 4:8).

The title of this book (with its two parts connected with a slash) expresses the fact that there is an intercausality between deep conversion and deep prayer. Each one brings about the other. An example on the human level: If a man loves a woman authentically and profoundly (I am not speaking of the media version of love), he would not for a moment entertain the idea of harming her, or of tainting the beauty of her chastity. People intimate with God resist with all their might not only deadly sins, which kill the relationship, but also venial transgressions which, if deliberate, cool it.

Jesus and his Mother needed no conversion. They were sinless. So also they enjoyed the most sublime prayer union with each other and with the Father and the Holy Spirit —he as the divine Son and she as the most blessed of all mothers. Hence, it is no surprise that he habitually spent long solitudes absorbed in the most profound communion with the Father (Lk 5:16), long before dawn (Mk 1:35), even all through the night (Lk 6:12). She as his Mother incessantly pondered the word in her heart (Lk 2:19, 51), and led the apostles in continuous prayer for forty days in preparation for the coming of the Holy Spirit (Acts 1:14). To see in greater detail why and how intimacy and conversion are intertwined the reader may consult *Fire Within*.

Be Humble

It may not be immediately apparent to everyone how this virtue is indispensable for both conversion and for prayer in any depth. It may well seem that if a person lives faithfully the Be's we have already considered, profound conversion is assured. Yes, that is true, but all the same, humility offers practical know-how in solving wisely the thousands of nitty-gritty problems that come up in anyone's life, and especially in one who is trying to avoid even small selfishnesses. I refer to the insight and light we need to choose prudently the better paths in the endless multiplicities we daily encounter. These last two sentences are seldom explained and illustrated. We shall do both.

We begin with a few comments about what humility is. Two words say it well. Humility is complete honesty—not just partial candor, but full. We have gifts, yes, but we also have limitations and defects. We know perhaps many things, but we are ignorant of far more things. This is true of all scholars in all specialties. It is laughable how highly competent scientists can pontificate about metaphysical questions without seeming to know that they are using metaphysical principles. The very best scholars, whether they are physicists or theologians, have a good grasp of how much they do not know even in their own field, let alone those outside of it.

Humility is full honesty in other ways as well. We may acknowledge that we have made some progress in holiness, but most likely there are some remaining egocentrisms. And all of us have experienced failures and made many mistakes. These also we should acknowledge. Especially we should be vividly aware that "every good and perfect gift comes from the Father of lights" (Jas 1:17). Or as Saint Paul puts it, "What have you that you did not receive?" (1 Cor 4:7). Everything you and I have that is beautiful, insightful or successful is a gift of God. To be acutely aware of this is to be humble and grateful.

Now how does this honesty promote conversion and prayer? Humility invites light, divine light that we otherwise would not have. Because God never forces himself on anyone, because he gives only if we really desire, he grants his light only to those who want it. If I am full of my own ideas, if in my mind I am always right, he backs off. As we earlier noted, on one occasion and filled with joy at the very thought of what he was going to say, Jesus said, "I bless you, Father, Lord of heaven and of earth, for hiding these things from the learned and the clever [the conceited] and revealing them to mere children. Yes, Father, for that is what it pleased you to do" (Lk 10:21 JB).

To choose wisely in the multiplicities of life we need the light given in the virtue of prudence, and this light the Lord loves to give to the humble, the little ones. Examples abound: How to be both firm and gentle . . . When to make a well-founded exception to a human law and when not . . . How to live gospel frugality in marriage or priesthood . . . How to decide wisely among apostolic opportunities when one cannot accept them all . . . When and how to admonish son or daughter or peer or husband or wife . . . Whether to fast and to what extent . . . How in concrete circumstances to "live a life of love" (2 Jn 6 JB) . . . How to combine contemplation and action, neglecting neither . . . How to be bold and humble at the same time . . . Caring for the family and giving to the poor . . . How to fit magnanimity and humility into one's course of action . . . Showing warmth and chastity together. We should notice the frequency of the word "how" occurring in these examples. Precisely how to further our conversion in the vast multiplicities of life is immensely important. Hence one of the many benefits of humility is the light found in the virtue of prudence, the virtue that aids us in applying the beauty of gospel principles to the immense number of details in the life of each of us.

Be Specific

The sixth element in our practical program turns our attention in another way to the nitty-gritty details of human life

—which, of course, is the only way we can live a human life. Vague, general and grandiose aspirations do not produce conversion, let alone deep conversion. Velleities are common: "I wish I were better . . . I'd like to get rid of my overeating or my bursts of impatience or my gossiping . . . or my more or less unchaste use of television . . . or my . . ." The list could go on and on. "I really do want to be better, but nothing lasting happens."

If well-meaning generalities produce slim results, is there anything else that needs to be done to get rid of sins, mortal and venial? Anything in addition to what we have already noted? Yes, it is to be rid of mere vague wishes. We need to focus on clear and specific aims and plans. An analogy with modern warfare may be helpful here. High-level military officers plan their ground, air and sea campaigns in fine detail—including alternative responses to differing situations and responses of the enemy. The best officers leave little to chance. What we read of contemporary tactics confirms this.

The spiritual life is, as Job 7:1 reminded us, a warfare. Vague wishes go nowhere. This is why many of the wise religious orders retain the practice they call particular examen. It is exactly what its name indicates. In this exercise the person focuses special daily attention on one fault to be corrected or one virtue to be acquired or improved upon: gossiping, overeating or bursts of temper, for example; or gentleness, humility or truth telling. At the same time each day (an aid to remembrance), in a prayerful atmosphere and place, this individual goes over the previous twenty-four hours, examining how he behaved on the one specific point. He notices how he succeeded or fell with regard to that one aim, what were the times and circumstances, who were the persons who triggered the successes or failures. Most likely it will not be many days before he sees a pattern emerging (if he did not already know it). This first part of particular examen can be done in one or two minutes.

Then he spends another short time planning for the next twenty-four hours and preparing to do better on this one point. It is wise to begin particular examen with a short prayer for light to know oneself better, and to conclude it with another for vigilance and readiness aimed at success in execution. This whole exercise can be done in a few minutes. Its helpfulness is due to putting concern and determination into practice.

Bernard Bro, O.P., in his study of Saint Thérèse of Lisieux, offers a concrete example of how this saint went about acquiring a specific virtue and avoiding a potential fault. She did not simply wish in general to love her religious sisters. She selected a specific need for improvement, foresaw the time, persons and circumstances in which she was going to meet the problem:

> Thérèse had acquired the habit of smiling every time when, at work, she was disturbed by a Sister who came with or without reason, to ask her for some service. She noted this with humor in her last manuscript. She was ready for annoyance: "I want it; I count on it . . . so I am always happy" (*Saint Thérèse of Lisieux*, p. 62).

That is particular examen in a nutshell and in action. This charming saint was concerned, determined, motivated, much in love, deeply prayerful and specific. It is no wonder she so quickly reached heroic holiness and the transforming intimacy with the Trinity indwelling. She was living the surefire program, even if she did not hear of it put in those words.

Be Persevering

It is comparatively easy for most of us to do something difficult for a day or two, but it is less likely that we will be faithful to our resolution for a month or two. And very few indeed will sacrifice comfort and ease for years on end—unless they are deeply in love, real love. As we have noted, our surefire program brings great happiness in one's state in life, whether that be priesthood, convent, monastery or marriage. Even when people read or hear of this happy result, seldom do they perseveringly follow the hard road and the narrow gate that lead to a blessed life and joy (Mt 7:13–14). To say this is simply to recall in other words our earlier discussion of the remarkable resistance most people place before deep conversion.

An unfortunate but frequent problem that follows after making a retreat or a parish mission is that initial enthusiasm slowly wanes as the days and weeks pass by. This experience can be personally discovered by asking oneself a year after an excellent retreat or mission: "Have I grown significantly in the last twelve months? How precisely have I changed for the better? Have I stopped snapping at others, or have I given up gossiping or overeating? Am I now faithful to my period of daily meditative/contemplative communing with the Lord?"

Faithfully implementing our program of Be's should, of course, further persevering effort, but two more helps can provide assurance that the program may continue. The first is a personal weekly checkup. We are assuming here that the person has written down the seven Be's lest important elements in the program be forgotten. Our suggestion here is that once a week at the same time (lest it be forgotten), we go over our plan, one Be at a time, "Am I faithful to each of these seven factors? How am I succeeding—or failing? Do I need to change anything in order to improve or correct what is amiss?"

A second help can serve as a backup, if for some reason the first is not achieving its purpose fully enough: periodic accountability to someone reliable. This could be one's confessor or spiritual director. Or, when it may be feasible, spouses in an ideal marriage could agree to be accountable to each other—even to the point of gently calling the other to task when such may be helpful. What we have in mind here is poles apart in spirit, in motivation and in execution from the bane of continuous faultfinding, complaining, scolding, nagging. In religious orders this practice of voluntary accountability is sometimes called monition, an agreed upon and welcomed admonishing of one another done in a spirit of mutual love, and at mutually suitable time and place. The New Testament speaks expressly of this type of loving another person: "Teach and admonish one another in all wisdom" (Col 3:16).

Our Program: an Overview

We may take it to be clear that our first four Be's are a closely knit unity. Each one implies the others. There are no gimmicks. These motivations and practices will be found together or not at all. Only people with a growing contemplative intimacy with God will be falling in love. Only they who are falling in love will be determined to be effective in getting rid of offenses to their supreme Beloved. Only they will be lastingly concerned about this "one thing", this whole process of profound and lasting transformation.

Conversely, only if we are sincerely concerned about our

lack of progress, will we be determined to ponder our motivation and prayer depth—and then do something about them. We are then less likely to permit ourselves to forget any of the Be's or to take our eyes off Jesus and his salvific message, the mainspring of the entire enterprise.

That our last three Be's are necessary from the practical point of view seems so obvious that a further explanation seems superfluous. We may however conclude this chapter with a personal experience.

In my extensive vagabonding for the Lord over several decades, I have had the blessing of meeting a goodly number of interesting and edifying people. In one recent summer session on a college campus, I was giving a concentrated course for the general public on contemplative prayer. In the front row of the classroom was a Pentagon general (we were in the Washington, D.C. area). This was surprise enough in itself, but still more so was his assiduous note-taking during the lectures. One day he asked if I would have lunch with him in the college cafeteria. I gladly agreed, and when we met he brought along his briefcase. Over lunch we discussed course content, he wishing to get from it as much as possible. In passing I learned that his present job in the Pentagon was planning battles for the armed services. It seems to me that this also was what he was about in attending our course. This rather unusual student was apparently applying to the battle of life our series of Be's—though without that vocabulary.

10

THE SACRAMENTAL DIMENSION

Our surefire plan is not yet quite complete. We have noticed that it is a combination of divine grace and our cooperation with it, both absolutely indispensable. In carrying out this plan we are heeding Jesus' admonition to Angela of Foligno: "Make yourself a capacity, and I will make myself a torrent" —a profoundly biblical idea.

Yet there is another dimension to this enterprise, namely, the sacraments, especially the Eucharist and Penance (Reconciliation). The risen Lord in the Mass and in his Real Presence in the tabernacle is, through his Holy Spirit, the source of all life, all saintliness in the Church. Our renewal of the Paschal Mystery at the altar is the summit of each of our days on this earthly pilgrimage. Because we have a wealth of literature on this subject, magisterial, theological and popular, I refer the reader to these rich sources. (See especially the *Catechism of the Catholic Church*, nos. 1135–99; 1322–419.) Less has been done in the pastoral catechizing of the faithful on how to profit more fully from the sacrament of Reconciliation, especially from the point of view of deepening conversion.

We may begin by recalling what we explained in Chapter 5, "Remarkable resistance", about how common it seems to be among the faithful that people can go to confession regularly, and yet decade after decade confess the same venial sins without any notable improvement. Gossiping, overeating, laziness, willed impatience, harmful use of the media are among many possible illustrations. Confessing these sins or others like them over and over again often seems to have little or no visible effect on their occurrence. This phenomenon cannot be due to a lack in the sacrament of Reconciliation —or of the Eucharist, which the people of whom we are speaking may receive weekly or even daily. Lack of results must be due to deficiencies in serious efforts at real conversion or else to receiving these sacraments in a routine, mediocre, slovenly manner.

So we ask how should a person prepare for and receive this sacrament of Penance in order to further deepening conversion and prayer? Some of the answers to this question many of us have heard in our early catechism classes, but have we forgotten them? Others we may not have heard at all, or with insufficient clarity of explanation.

Outlook on the Sacrament

First of all, we must emphasize that this sacrament is for guilt, not for mere feelings or mistakes. Simply to feel impatient or angry or envious are not sins, because there is no free will in a mere feeling. We usually cannot control emotions, at least not completely, and hence there is little or no guilt in them. And if there is no guilt, there is nothing to confess, no sin. What we do need to confess to the priest are things we can control but do not: raising our voice, snapping at another, overeating, gossiping, harshness, knowingly to linger on immodest television scenes or media photos.

Further, ordinary forgetfulness and mistakes are not to be

confessed: for example, forgetting on a Friday in Lent and eating meat. Once again there is no guilt in that case. Nor should a person confined to bed by illness confess missing Mass on a Sunday. One of the reasons we should not confess non-guilt items is that they distract us from what we can and should correct: real guilt, real sins.

In this chapter we are dealing with things we can control, faults we can and should get rid of in a deepening conversion. And we must emphasize also that merely confessing guilty deeds or omissions is not enough. There are people who seem to assume that the routine mentioning of faults in the sacrament of Penance without a serious intention to stop them is sufficient. They confess overeating or gossiping or vanity decade after decade with no real decision, "I am going to take steps to stop this." The "firm purpose of amendment" part of genuine sorrow, sincere contrition, seems to be absent. Of course there is then no progress toward real conversion. Jesus in all his tender mercy did also say, "Go and sin no more." We can see now more clearly how this sacrament fits intimately into our surefire program.

At this point a practical question can arise, a good question serious people can have: suppose we are not sure whether we gave in with our will in showing impatience . . . Or we are doubtful as regards overeating whether we were aware at the time that it was too much? When we are not sure of guilt, the doubt should be briefly mentioned in our confession: for example, I *may* have been partially guilty in showing anger, or I may have been slow in turning away from an unchaste scene on television.

Another valid question good people can easily have: suppose since one's last confession there is nothing to mention that had certain, sure guilt? In this case the penitent should

confess again some past guilt-laden fault that surely did occur, and he confesses it with continuing sorrow. There cannot be a sacrament of Reconciliation unless real guilt is confessed. Even though the sin was forgiven the first time the
penitent was absolved, the Church's power given by Jesus
continues to heal and give grace.

Hence, the main element in preparing to receive the sacrament of Penance is genuine sorrow, the firm commitment
to change, to take concrete steps to correct what one is confessing: "Go and sin no more."

It follows then that ordinarily this sacrament is not in-
tended to be a counseling session about difficult human relations. The confessor of course often does well to advise
the penitent briefly on how to avoid a given sin. But in-
terrelational problems usually should be discussed outside
of the confessional setting. People who want to be healed
of their guilt should not be kept waiting at length for non-
sacramental reasons. This observation calls for further explanation, which we now pursue.

The "Few Confessions Crisis"

It is common today to hear people speaking of the alarming
increase in the numbers of the faithful who seldom or never
go to confession. No one supposes that the reason is that
our contemporaries are more virtuous than our ancestors in
the faith. Far more likely explanations are mainly threefold:
(1) a loss of the sense of sin; (2) doctrinal and moral dissent
among some theologians and priests; and (3) the widespread
and unmet need for conversion, deep conversion.

But there are other factors as well. While some priests
continue to hear many confessions, others hear few. Some

priests are knowledgeable, devoted, faithful, prayerful, gentle confessors—and people flock to them. They generously give hours each week to the taxing and tiring martyrdom of the confessional, of which the Curé of Ars and Padre Pio are models. They promote this sacrament from the pulpit, and they make themselves available. Other priests lack these traits, and they give little time to this service of the faithful. They attract few penitents. They are not models of priestly zeal.

Then, too, it is widely spoken of and admitted that there is a lack of leadership among some bishops. We may recall once again the penetrating comment of Pope John Paul II to bishops making their *ad limina* visit to the Holy See: "Your first duty as pastors is not projects and organizations, but to lead your people to a deep intimacy with the Trinity." To lead in this context means, of course, to lead first by living an example of deep contemplative prayer and then to teach what they themselves are living. Our best people are thirsting for this quality of leadership. I have been coming into contact with their expressions of this desire in retreat and lecture work over several decades. Many of our best people do not think it is being met.

The Problem of Prolixity

True as all of the above is, we need to consider here a problem, which to my knowledge has not been addressed by pastors, even though members of the flock at times complain about it. It is a deeper problem than superficial observation would suggest. I refer to penitents who take undue amounts of time in what they have to say to the confessor. To some people this may appear to be much ado about nothing, or at least nothing much. To others it could seem simply a complaint of priests who want to leave the confessional as soon as they can. Both of these views indicate that those who hold them have not thought much about the matter.

In what we are saying here, we have in mind normal parishes of perhaps 1,500 to 2,000 families. We are not thinking of a retired priest who can give twenty or thirty minutes in an appointment arrangement. If all priests were generous and promoted frequent confession by example and by word, and even if only a small percentage of the faithful went to confession as they ought, most parish priests would be overwhelmed by the many hours they would have to spend in the confessional, especially if penitents commonly take four or five minutes (or more) to say what could be said in a minute or two. The usual priest's many other time-consuming duties would have to be curtailed or omitted. At the same time the prolixity of many penitents keeps others in the line waiting for much longer than is necessary. Not surprisingly, some people, perhaps more than we suspect, avoid the confessional because of the long delays others unnecessarily cause. One woman recently remarked to me that she just doesn't go to confession for this reason.

Perhaps the best way to begin our case for brevity on the part of the penitent (who actually is each one of us) is to recall the examples of the two sainted models for ideal confessors, the Curé of Ars and Padre Pio. Both of these marvelous priests were able to come to the aid of untold thousands of sinners because they required their penitents to be brief. The long lines would have otherwise been impossible. To get the point one need only imagine the Curé on an average day beginning at one in the morning and sitting all day in his tiny box for thirteen or fourteen hours, as inconsiderate people kept others waiting as they narrated details unnecessary for the confession of their own sins, let alone trying to confess those of others. He did not allow it. In a healthy parish there should be many confessions throughout a year. Brevity of the penitents is, therefore, of critical importance if this sacrament is to be received as it ought to be—for the reasons we shall consider a bit further on. Hence, we wish to explain (1) How the penitent can be brief and yet accurate; (2) Examples of being clear and yet brief; (3) Reasons for brevity.

How To Be Brief, Clear and Accurate

We can offer four guides to further this idea. The first is that the penitent confess guilt, not mere feelings or mistakes—as we have already explained. The second is that one avoids mentioning the failings and faults of others, for example, the other person's part in an argument, what they did or said that triggered the penitent's outburst of anger. The confessor knows that there are two sides to most conflicts—let the adversary confess his own sins. Thirdly, one should confess only the essentials of the sin, not a history of what took place, not unnecessary details. Lastly, do not repeat two or three times what has already been said once. If something is not clear, the confessor can ask about it.

Examples of Brevity in Confessing Specific Sins

The reader should notice that these illustrations do not express feelings but rather acts of the will, things the sinner could have chosen to avoid, but did not: "I showed impatience . . . I gossiped . . . I showed grouchiness . . . I

was harsh, not gentle . . . I ate too much . . . I was lazy
. . . I wasted time with television . . . I watched immodest
scenes deliberately . . . We used contraceptives . . . I mas-
turbated. . . ." For mortal sins the number of times must be
mentioned, as Jesus himself implied. In sins against chastity
the penitent should add whether he is single or married.
These few illustrations make it clear that a completely correct confession can ordinarily be done in a minute or two
—or even less. We are presuming, of course, that the sinner has spent enough time in examining his conscience, so
that when he enters the confessional he well knows what
to confess and how to be brief about it.

Why Should the Penitent Be Brief?

We have explained the basic reason for brevity, but still
more needs to be said. We ask the reader to notice that our
reasons are all for the penitent's benefit, and for the many
others who need the priest's services in a large number of
other diverse and pressing ways. Hence we should notice
several other considerations.

In our busy and pressured world, every worthy business
or medical or governmental agency tries its best to minimize
the time people must wait for its services. Many people have
important things to do besides waiting in line unnecessarily.
Brevity is being considerate of others and their needs, just
as we would like them to be such toward us.

Further, in the matter of getting our sins sacramentally absolved there is a special urgency that we do not keep others
from receiving this sacrament through our own prolixity. I
would not want this charge brought against me on judgment
day.

Then, too, the person who focuses on his own sins, rather

than on those with whom he lives and works, is more likely to correct them, to face his real guilt more honestly and then to do something effective about it. On the other hand, those who speak much about the faults of others, often repeating themselves in the process, tend to minimize their own defects.

One may say at this point, "Well, cannot the confessor just admonish the penitent to be brief for all these reasons? They surely make sense." Yes, they do make sense, but the confessor is trying to be gentle, and there are people who are easily offended even by a gentle admonition. Some may even decide not to go to confession again if the priest suggests they are taking too much time. It is therefore much better for parish priests to give homilies explaining all these things, for then there is less danger of people feeling hurt by even a kindly individual request.

A further benefit from brevity is that it gives the confessor a bit of time to offer needed advice about correcting the guilty deeds that have been mentioned. Penitents who talk much exert a pressure on the priest to omit what he should say to them. The pressure here of course refers both to the long line of others seeking absolution, and to the other ways in which the priest is expected to serve the faithful that day.

This brings us to our final reason for brevity. In a typically large and lively parish, there is a whole list of other time-consuming duties the clergy must care for, in addition to hearing confessions and to celebrating the daily Eucharistic liturgy with their people. Among these demands on the priest's time are: Preparing homilies and other instructions . . . Visiting the sick and offering them the sacraments . . . Caring for consultations and other appointments of a dozen different types . . . Attending meetings of parish organizations and apostolic services in addition to those concerned with diocesan commitments . . . Marriage preparation and instruction classes . . . His own continuing studies all his lifetime . . . just as a medical doctor must do if he is to remain competent in his field . . . Caring for funeral preparations and Masses (and conducting the cemetery services and attending the family luncheon afterwards) . . . Letters to answer, not to mention phone calls at any time of day and night . . . His own personal prayer life of the Liturgy of the Hours, meditation/contemplation, spiritual reading (these alone take two or three hours each day in the life of the faithful priest—and the faithful need that he be this kind of priest). In all these duties he is simply obeying the gospel and the mind of the Church. We should not forget either that it is this kind of shepherd who does immeasurably more good for his flock, than the one who gives little or no time to a deepening intimacy with the Trinity. One can easily see that this statement is not an exaggeration simply by reading the lives of the Church's most effective bishops and priests: Saints Augustine, John Chrysostom, Bernard, Francis, Dominic, Ignatius, Robert Bellarmine, the Curé of Ars and Padre Pio—and a host of others. Pope John Paul II remarked that "the Pope's first duty is prayer." And best of all there is the example of the Master who habitually spent hours per day ("long before dawn" . . . "all night") absorbed in the deepest prayer communion with his Father (see Mk 1:35; Lk 5:16; 6:12, etc.).

In view of all these considerations, it should be easy to see how unbecoming (to put it mildly) it is for people to go on and on in unneeded details and repetitions whether it is in the confessional or in other consultations and telephone calls.

Frequency of Confession

Somewhat related to our present discussion is the question of how often it is recommended that the faithful receive the sacrament of Penance. The Church's official answer to this question is found in Canon no. 989. All the faithful who have reached the age of discretion are obliged to confess their sins (if grave) at least once a year. Religious, "desiring closer union with God, should endeavor to receive the sacrament of penance frequently, that is twice a month." Superiors "should encourage them in this effort and should make it possible for the members to go to confession at least every two weeks and even oftener, if they wish to do so" (Congregation for Consecrated Life, *Decree on Confession for Religious*, no. 3). Hence, weekly confession is not required of religious.

In most places in the Church today, the shortage of priests and the problem of clerical burnout can make very frequent confession by many of the faithful practically impossible except in the case of priests who are retired or otherwise released from ordinary duties. The mere mention of the priests' obligations above makes this clear.

There is another consideration that should be kept in mind in a person's deciding to receive this sacrament very frequently. One is the danger that the practice may become a routine and repetitious habit with little change toward deeper conversion, toward getting rid of willed sins. Religious superiors should not make a rule of weekly confession so that members decide they need to go to confession merely because "I am supposed to go". It would be better to receive the sacrament once a month with a real determination to change for the better.

We may close this chapter on confession and conversion

with a currently popular contrition formula which accurately summarizes much of what we have considered as theologically essential. I shall take the liberty to emphasize the indispensable elements in genuine sorrow. We should notice also what is not mentioned as part of confession, as well as what is so clearly brought out:

> My God, I am *sorry* for my *sins with all my heart*. In *choosing* to do wrong and failing to do good, I have *sinned* against you whom I should love above all things. *I firmly intend*, with your help, to do penance, *to sin no more*, and *to avoid whatever leads me to sin*. Our Savior Jesus Christ suffered and died for us. In his name, my God, have mercy. Amen.

Every word in this act of genuine contrition is important, of course. The ideas italicized bring out clearly much of the content of this chapter. A person who lives this simple but beautiful prayer has a mighty help to deep conversion and deep intimacy with the Trinity.

POSTSCRIPT

Even though the details involved in the intercausality between deep conversion and deep prayer may seem to be numerous, the whole transforming process is uncomplicated and beautifully simple. Yes, there are details, and it has taken us ten chapters to explain them. But after all life is made up of countless situations and specific decisions, all of them unique for each person. No one becomes an excellent mother or father, priest or scientist, nurse or surgeon, scholar or technician in a month or two—probably not in most cases in a decade or two. We are developing beings, not angels.

One of the joys of achieving excellence in the loftier realities of life, such as art or science or theology, is the delight found in intellectually seeing and experiencing the richness of each field's unity, harmony and beauty. And perceiving the resplendence and harmony of their interrelationships, each field with the others, brings additional delight. Hans Urs von Balthasar was on target: truth is indeed symphonic.

Among all worldviews it is the gospel alone that produces the beauty of the saints. Nothing else does. They are deeply converted, and therefore utterly in love with triune Beauty. Even though our surefire program is cast in contemporary thought patterns and terminology, it is pure gospel. As we have noted, this plan contains no gimmicks, no pop psychology. Clever phrases and shallow ideas do not, and cannot produce the splendor of profound intimacy with anyone, least of all with the radiance of Father, Son and Holy Spirit—our eternal enthrallment. This unspeakable destiny of the beatific vision in our risen body lies beyond comparison with the sacrifices we make in living the admittedly demanding program of our seven Be's. "What no eye has seen, nor ear heard, nor the heart of man conceived, what God has prepared for those who love him" (1 Cor 2:9).

BIBLIOGRAPHY

Bloom, Alan. *The Closing of the American Mind*. New York: Simon and Schuster, 1987.

Bro, Fr. Bernard. *Saint Thérèse of Lisieux: Her Family, Her God, Her Message*. San Francisco: Ignatius Press, 2003.

Catechism of the Catholic Church. Second edition. Vatican City: Libreria Editrice Vaticana, 1997.

Chesterton, G. K. *The Everlasting Man*. San Francisco: Ignatius Press, 1993.

Dubay, Thomas. *Caring: A Biblical Theology of Community*. Denville, N.Y.: Dimension Books, 1973.

———. *Evidential Power of Beauty*. San Francisco: Ignatius Press, 1999.

———. *Fire Within*. San Francisco: Ignatius Press, 1989.

———. *Happy Are You Poor*. San Francisco: Ignatius Press, 2002.

———. *Prayer Primer*. San Francisco: Ignatius Press, 2002.

John of the Cross. *The Ascent of Mount Carmel* in the *Collected Works of St. John of the Cross*, trans. Kieran Kavanaugh, O.C.D., and Otilio Rodriguez, O.C.D., Washington, D.C.: ICS Publications, 1973.

Knox, Ronald. *Enthusiasm*. New York: Oxford University Press, 1961.

Lewis, C. S. *God in the Dock*. Grand Rapids, Mich.: Eerd-mans, 1970.

Pearce, Joseph. *Literary Converts*. San Francisco: Ignatius Press, 2000.

Sheed, Frank. *The Church and I*. Garden City, N.Y.: Dou-bleday, 1974.

Von Balthasar, Hans Urs. *Truth Is Symphonic*. San Francisco: Ignatius Press, 1987.